Praise for *Holistic Accountability: Serving Students, Schools, and Community*

There is no concept in education that is used more and understood less than accountability. In *Holistic Accountability,* Douglas Reeves brings clarity and understanding to the concept. This book should be read and its recommendations followed by anyone seriously attempting to make sense of this buzzword.

> Lawrence W. Lezotte, Ph.D.
> Education Consultant and Commentator
> Effective Schools Products, Ltd.
> Okemos, MI

Douglas Reeves's practical approach to assessment and accountability provides a clear picture of the interaction between leadership, assessment, teaching, and the learning process. The holistic accountability cycle serves as a blueprint for making accountability a constructive force for improving teaching and learning.

> Karen Young, President
> NSCI and Learning 24/7
> Phoenix, AZ

Douglas Reeves knows education—not from an ivory tower perspective, but from that of a committed practitioner. His work provides a refreshingly constructive take on the issue of accountability: Data should be used to guide learning, instruction, and educational policy, not to punish students or teachers.

> Jeff Howard, President
> Efficacy Institute
> Lexington, MA

Douglas Reeves makes sense of the hodgepodge of issues that currently surround educational accountability. The concepts related to accountability are turned into practical applications that not only address the concerns of school personnel and community members, but also, more importantly, focus on improving student achievement.

> Deanna Housfeld, Director (Retired)
> Department of Research and Assessment
> Milwaukee Public Schools, WI

This book is a great practitioner's guide to improving student achievement through accountability. I agree accountability is more than test scores. Douglas Reeves has taken a very challenging topic of accountability and has made it very user friendly. He focuses on the true mission of education, which is improving student learning. Accountability is much more than tests scores, as Reeves points out in this outstanding book.

> Terry J. Thompson
> Superintendent of Schools
> The Metropolitan School District of Wayne Township
> Indianapolis, IN

To the memory of
Jean Brooks Reeves

—D. B. Reeves

HOLISTIC
ACCOUNTABILITY

EXPERTS IN ASSESSMENT™

SERIES EDITORS
THOMAS R. GUSKEY AND ROBERT J. MARZANO

8-BOOK SET: D1800-0-7619-7874-7 (PAPER)

HOLISTIC ACCOUNTABILITY

SERVING STUDENTS, SCHOOLS, AND COMMUNITY

DOUGLAS B. REEVES

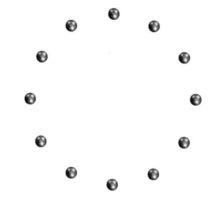

EXPERTS IN ASSESSMENT ™

SERIES EDITORS
THOMAS R. GUSKEY AND ROBERT J. MARZANO

CORWIN PRESS, INC.
A Sage Publications Company
Thousand Oaks, California

For information:

Corwin Press, Inc.
A Sage Publications Company
2455 Teller Road
Thousand Oaks, California 91320
E-mail: order@corwinpress.com

Sage Publications Ltd.
6 Bonhill Street
London EC2A 4PU
United Kingdom

Sage Publications India Pvt. Ltd.
M-32 Market
Greater Kailash I
New Delhi 110 048 India

Printed in the United States of America

Library of Congress Cataloging-in-Publication Data

Reeves, Douglas B., 1953-
  Holistic accountability: Serving students, schools, and community /
by Douglas B. Reeves.
    p. cm. — (Experts in assessment™)
  Includes bibliographical references and index.
    ISBN 0-7619-7831-3 (c : alk. paper) — ISBN 0-7619-7832-1 (p : alk.
paper)
    1. Educational accountability—United States. 2. Academic
achievement—United States. 3. Educational tests and
measurements—United States.   I. Title. II. Series.
  LB2806.22 .R46 2001
  379.1'58—dc21   2001002906

This book is printed on acid-free paper.

01 02 03 04 05 10 9 8 7 6 5 4 3 2 1

Acquiring Editor: Rachel Livsey
Corwin Editorial Assistant: Phyllis Cappello
Production Editor: Diane S. Foster
Editorial Assistant: Ester Marcelino
Typesetter/Designer: Rebecca Evans
Copy Editor: Amy Kazilsky
Proofreader: Joyce Kuhn
Indexer: Will Ragsdale
Cover Designer: Tracy E. Miller

Contents

About the Author

D r. Douglas B. Reeves is the chairman and founder of the International Center for Educational Accountability, a nonprofit organization, and the Center for Performance Assessment. He works with school systems throughout the world on the issues of standards, assessment, and accountability. He is the author of 10 books, and a frequent keynote speaker on leadership issues. He can be reached at the Center offices at (800) 844-6599 or via e-mail at dreeves@makingstandardswork.com.

Series Editors' Introduction

Standards, assessment, accountability, and grading—these are the issues that dominated discussions of education in the 1990s. Today, they are at the center of every modern education reform effort. As educators turn to the task of implementing these reforms, they face a complex array of questions and concerns that little in their background or previous experience has prepared them to address. This series is designed to help in that challenging task.

In selecting the authors, we went to individuals recognized as true experts in the field. The ideas of these scholar-practitioners have already helped shape current discussions of standards, assessment, accountability, and grading. But equally important, their work reflects a deep understanding of the complexities involved in implementation. As they developed their books for this series, we asked them to extend their thinking, to push the edge, and to present new perspectives on what should be done and how to do it. That is precisely what they did. The books they crafted provide not only cutting-edge perspectives but also practical guidelines for successful implementation.

We have several goals for this series. First, that it be used by teachers, school leaders, policymakers, government officials, and all those concerned with these crucial aspects of education reform. Second, that it helps broaden understanding of the complex issues involved in standards, assessment, accountability, and grading. Third, that it leads to more thoughtful policies and programs. Fourth, and most important, that it helps accomplish the basic goal for which all reform initiatives are intended—namely, to enable all students to learn excellently and to gain the many positive benefits of that success.

— *Thomas R. Guskey*
— *Robert J. Marzano*
Series Editors

Introduction

Accountability in education is inevitable. The choice for educational and community leaders is not whether to have accountability. Instead, these leaders must decide how to make this slippery concept effective and fair. In the pages that follow, you will find a step-by-step guide for creating a holistic accountability system that will improve student achievement, create a motivated and professionally engaged staff, and transform accountability from an emotionally laden and destructive term to one that is constructive and rational.

The need for accountability could not be more pronounced. Political forces demand it and a growing number of school systems are making the word "accountability" a primary theme of everything from teacher negotiations to leadership decisions to student promotion. The very word accountability evokes strong emotional reactions both from advocates and from critics. Accountability advocates are typically those who have grown impatient with the slow progress of many schools and who believe that continued toleration of mediocrity and excuses denies educational opportunity to children. Accountability critics express fear for the victims of accountability. These victims, in the views of accountability critics, include children denied promotion, teachers denied tenure, and principals terminated from their leadership positions all because of test score performance.

Thus the debate over educational accountability is dominated by two extreme and unproductive views. At one extreme are those who, claiming to focus on results, equate accountability with a litany of test scores. At the other extreme are those who, despairing of all the variables outside school that affect student achievement, claim that accountability is futile and that, all things considered, teachers and administrators are doing about as well as can be expected. Each side accuses the other of failure to understand or, as the rhetorical wars escalate, care about children. *Holistic Accountability* offers a practical response to this challenge.

How You Can Use This Book

Educational accountability has traditionally been the province of state and district policymakers, and without question, legislators and board members can influence accountability systems for the better if they take a broader view of the purpose and scope of educational accountability policies. Nevertheless, this book has a much wider audience than policymakers. Educators, administrators, school leaders, and parents can make an immediate and profound impact on educational accountability policies in individual schools through the use of the principles of holistic accountability. It is not necessary to have a change in state accountability policy for individual schools and classrooms to improve their focus on the causes of improved student achievement. You can use this book to change the agenda of the next meeting of your Parent-Teacher Association or School Accountability Committee from an isolated discussion of test scores to a broad and deep consideration of the antecedents of excellence. You can use this book to improve the quality of the test report you receive from the assessment office through the consideration of additional variables beyond test scores, ethnicity, and family economic status. You can use this book to improve the quality of your next staff development program so that the impact of specific teaching strategies, assessment practices, and curricula can be considered in a systematic manner. Indeed, you can use this book to avoid any prospective teaching technique that carries the intimation of "flavor of the month" rather than a substantive contribution to student learning. You can use this book to improve the dialogue between parents and teachers so that the focus of the discussion moves beyond test scores and student performance to include the underlying causes of student achievement.

Most important, you can use this book to challenge the insidious notion that ethnicity and family economic status are the primary variables influencing student achievement. When a school, district, or state is able to analyze systematically a number of factors related to student achievement, including the role of teachers, leaders, and policymakers, then it forces the adults in the system to take greater responsibility for the educational results of the children. Only with a consideration of all these factors will all stakeholders in the system stop blaming children and the demographic characteristics of their families and cease the endless generation of excuses that are the hallmarks of too many discussions of educational accountability. Holistic accountability is about using information to improve learning, teaching, and policy making. It is not about easy answers or facile excuses.

Keys to Holistic Accountability

There are four keys to building a holistic accountability system: structure, collaboration, implementation, and communication. The first three chapters introduce the basic structure and rationale for building a holistic accountability system. Effective leaders must first discuss the principles and vision that guide the creation of an accountability system before they proceed to accountability methods. Chapter 4 deals with the imperative of community collaboration, embracing a variety of stakeholders in the creation of a meaningful and fair accountability system. Chapter 5 further builds the case for a collaborative approach to accountability, integrating accountability with previous work done in the vast majority of school systems on academic standards. If accountability is to be an enduring concept rather than just "one more program" that draws the inevitable sigh of contempt from veteran teachers and administrators, then it must be clear that the holistic accountability system will build on the strong foundations of academic standards and other effective strategies already in place in the schools. Chapters 6 and 7 address the details of implementation, providing a 10-step approach to implementing a holistic accountability system. The final key to holistic accountability is communication, the theme of Chapter 8.

Accountability is an evolving arena, fraught with danger but rife with opportunities for school leaders willing to approach it in a constructive manner. If you are willing to share your experiences on accountability matters, go to the web site of the International Center for Educational Accountability at www.edaccountability.org. You will find free downloads of articles and research on the subject of educational accountability. You can also share your experiences and ask questions of experts in the field.

Acknowledgments

This book would not be possible without the contributions of some extraordinary people who share my passion for fundamental fairness and accuracy in educational accountability.

My first thanks must go to the students, teachers, and leaders of the school systems used as case studies for this book: The Metropolitan School District of Wayne Township, Milwaukee Public Schools, and the Riverview Gardens School District. By allowing me to be an observer of, and occasionally a participant in, their success, they have given me the education that experience alone provides. I am particularly indebted to Dr. Terry Thompson, Dr. Karen Gould, and Dr. Phil Ehrheart, and their colleagues in Wayne Township; to Mr. Robert Jasna, Mrs. Barbara Horton, Dr. Deanna Housfeld, and Mr. Tim McElhatten of Milwaukee Public Schools; and to Dr. Chris Wright, Dr. Dennis Dorsey, Bobby Gines, and Maureen Clancy-May of Riverview Gardens.

Every idea, article, and book for which I receive undue credit is the product of my colleagues at the Center for Performance Assessment and the International Center for Educational Accountability. I am particularly indebted to Larry Ainsworth, Eileen Allison, Chris Benavides, Audrey Blackwell, Shana Chambers, Anne Fenske, Paul Kane, Debbie Kemp, Mary Krause, Michelle LePatner, Michele Lopez, Matt Mason, Leland Morrison, Terry Osner, Devon

Sheldon, Mike White, Amy Whited, and Nan Woodson. The insightful editing of Allison Wedell Schumacher transformed this book from conception to reality. The creative mind of Kevin Flaim of Flaim Originals in Cheyenne, Wyoming, helped bring to life the illustrations in Chapter 3. Rachel Livsey of Corwin Press provided enthusiastic support for this book and others in the "Experts in Assessment™" series.

Dr. Robert Marzano and Professor Tom Guskey are not old enough to be called "national treasures" but they have, in fact, fulfilled such a role. Their insight, intelligence, good humor, and hard work have illuminated the field of educational assessment and standards in a manner unequaled by their peers in academia or public education. A few footnotes and this acknowledgment are woefully insufficient recognition of the role these men have played in shaping my intellectual development and my specific ideas on educational accountability.

I am very lucky to have smart friends, loved ones, and mentors who inspire me even when they least expect it. Dr. Joyce Bales, Hunt Bonan, Dr. Jeff Howard, Professor Audrey Kleinsasser, Professor Alan Moore, Andy Reeves, Dr. Mike Schmoker, and the Honorable Ray Simon are all in this category, and I value their affection and friendship even more than their extraordinary intellect.

Finally, this list is incomplete without an acknowledgment of my heritage of educators, including my father, Professor J. B. Reeves, whose students called him "friend" as well as teacher; my mother, Julie Reeves, whose uncompensated teaching over the years demonstrates the truth of Wilde's inequality between the value of lessons and their cost; Laura Anderson Johnson, my grandmother, a teacher and school superintendent in the years before the First World War; and my grandfather, Sherman Vester Reeves, an elementary school teacher who, in 1906, was required to publish his test scores on his Arkansas teaching license. If one were to seek the genesis of effective educational accountability, the town of Green Forest in the northwest part of that beautiful state might be a good place to look.

Shelley, for whom no words can express my intellectual and emotional debt, is the light of my life. The other stars in this constellation are Brooks, Alex, Julia, and James. For their patience with my preoccupations, I can only offer my heartfelt thanks and ask their continued forbearance. Few kids have been asked to respond to the question "What did you do in school today?" with the intensive interrogation provided by this author. That they are willing to respond with answers more enlightening than "Nothin'" is more testimony to my children's endurance and the hard work of their teachers than to my interrogatory skill.

CHAPTER 1

What Is Holistic Accountability?

The Central Purpose of Accountability

The central purpose of accountability is the improvement of student achievement. However obvious this statement may seem, it excludes a number of other purposes with which accountability in the field of education is frequently associated. If the central purpose of educational accountability is the improvement of student achievement, then the purpose cannot be grading, ranking, labeling, sorting, humiliating, embarrassing, or otherwise conducting a political sideshow for the partisans who prefer that their rhetoric remains undiluted with evidence. Both sides in the acrimonious debate surrounding educational accountability have had the opportunity to substitute political zeal for facts. Those who oppose public education have found some accountability systems quite useful in validating their attacks. Some purported defenders of public education, however, do little to advance their cause by attacking accountability, testing, and standards, as if the absence of accountability would safeguard the institution. The resolution of this controversy is neither the use of accountability as a destructive force to shake up public education, nor is it the protection of school leaders and educators from uncomfortable truths. Rather, this book proposes an accountability system that is constructive, comprehensive, and useful: holistic accountability.

Holistic accountability includes not only effects but causes. It includes not only variables within the school but many factors that significantly influence student achievement. It includes not only scores from students but measurements of how teachers, school leaders, policymakers, and parents influence the education of children. It includes not only quantitative data but also the rich description that qualitative information provides.

The Structure of Accountability Systems: Fragmentary or Holistic?

The structure of an accountability system is inextricably linked to its purpose. There are two fundamental choices in the structure of accountability systems: fragmentary and holistic. Fragmentary systems are those that focus exclusively on a very limited set of variables, typically state test scores. In the rare instances in which variables beyond test scores are included in fragmentary accountability systems, these variables include factors such as the ethnicity, economic status, or location of the students. These fragmentary accountability systems send the unfortunate message to stakeholders that accountability is little more than the sum of test scores, and the other variables that are related to educational achievement are those that are beyond our control. After all, because one cannot change economic status or skin color, it is convenient to conclude that, however unfortunate the results may be, the children are doing just about as well as can be expected, and thus no additional effort by the adults in the system will make much of a difference. Although few state policymakers are ever so blunt in their expressions of low expectations of schoolchildren, the inescapable conclusion of most accountability systems is as follows: Tests are the only way to evaluate student achievement, students come to school with high or low ability, and there really is not much that we can do about it. As long as we publish the results, this slovenly reasoning goes, we have done our job with respect to educational accountability.

There is a better way. The fundamental argument of this book is that fragmentary accountability systems offer little more than an educational autopsy, a brief and inconsequential set of numbers that, at best, explain why the patient died. These results, however, shed little light on how to make the patient better. Few readers would regard a single number reported by a physician as a sufficient set of data to guide their physical improvement. Few policymakers would submit to brain surgery after a single number was placed in their medical report. They rarely hesitate, however, to make significant financial and political decisions based on fragmentary information when the subject of those decisions are schools, teachers, and children.

Under ordinary circumstances, we require thoroughly detailed information before making important decisions about our health or about our money. Even in the context of business, decision makers never focus exclusively on the "bottom line" but need information about the source, causes, and related variables that might influence the bottom line. The most influential practice in strategic management of business organizations in the past 10 years has been the development of the "balanced scorecard" (Kaplan & Norton, 1996, 2000) in which business leaders consider a variety of indicators beyond the bottom line to guide their decisions. Only in the field of education do we routinely accept a single number as a substitute for a complex set of variables.

Holistic accountability is a superior model for policymakers, educational leaders, and the general public. Just as the balanced scorecard provides superior information for business leaders, holistic accountability provides comprehensive information that can lead to better decisions by teachers, school leaders, and policymakers. Ultimately, the teaching and leadership decisions based on holistic accountability lead to improved student achievement and better allocation of resources.

The Elements of Holistic Accountability

A holistic accountability system includes information on student achievement. This book is not a polemic against testing or the use of achievement data. Rather, test data should be used in context. The appropriate context for test scores is not the facile association of test data with ethnicity and poverty. Test data must instead be associated with its antecedents: professional teaching practices, educational standards, curriculum, sorting strategies, leadership techniques, and resource allocation.

Student Achievement Data

States vary widely in the use of student achievement data. Some states rely exclusively on a multiple-choice test to represent what students know and are able to do. Other states make use of multiple-method assessments including multiple-choice, short answer, and essay responses from students. A very few districts and states use comprehensive student achievement information, such as a body of evidence. In these rare circumstances, a student is never evaluated based on a single indicator or score. Rather, decision makers have information collected over several years, including student performance assessments, test scores, demonstrations, experiments, and observations by a variety of independent evaluators. In such circumstances, student achievement is represented by a variety of data from several sources. Whether the ultimate decision is to grant a student credit and a diploma, or to deny a student credit and a diploma, the states and districts with abundant assessment data are on much firmer ground. Moreover, these states and districts recognize what every teacher and student understands: There is more than one way to "show what you know."

Standards and Curriculum

In addition to a variety of student achievement data, a holistic accountability system will also include information about the standards and curriculum of the schools. Although standards have been inextricably linked to the existence of testing, it is important to note that the foundation of the standards movement stands in stark contrast to the excessive and inappropriate use of the typical standardized test. The essence of educational standards is the comparison of a student performance to a standard rather than to other students. Thus the use of a norm-referenced standardized test to determine whether or not a student has met a standard is contradictory and absurd. Students can be above average and appear adequate in the context of the norm-referenced test and nevertheless fail to meet a standard. Moreover, a student can meet a standard and yet fall below the average of other students. The essence of a standards-based approach to education is the existence of an immutable target toward which teachers and students can aim their efforts. The target in a standards-based system is not "who beat whom" but, rather, what was achieved by each student.

Although it is true that the public has an interest in knowing the extent to which students have met standards, it is manifestly untrue that the best way to assess student success on standards is the use of a norm-referenced test. Rather, a body of evidence that includes a variety of assignments, assessments, performances, demonstrations, and other indications of student ability best assess student success in the achievement of standards.

Policymakers must know more than information about student performance. They must also understand the extent to which students have the opportunity to achieve a standard. This requires an inquiry into the standards themselves, the relationship between standards and assessments, and the relationship between standards and student curriculum. The modern high school offers an illustration of how the mere existence of standards and standards-based curriculum does not establish the opportunity for students to learn. Because we have a history of student choice in high school curricula, states have created the following bizarre situation: Standards require the achievement of certain levels of mastery in written expression and mathematics, along with requirements in science and social studies. State curriculum documents have been created that appear to match the state standards. In the most ideal circumstances, the state tests also match the curriculum and the standards. But the entire house of cards comes falling down if students have the opportunity to choose a less rigorous curriculum than that which is linked to the state standards and testing regime.

The American College Testing Program (Noble, 1999) found that the actual curriculum taken by students is far more influential in determining student success than demographic variables. This startling finding flies in the face of the common presumption that the primary variables affecting student performance are ethnicity and economics. In fact, school leaders and policy-makers must take personal responsibility for the results that students achieve if the policies of schools allow students to be denied the opportunity to achieve standards. Ironically, this may involve reducing a student's opportunity to make inappropriate curriculum decisions. It is, nevertheless, absurd to elevate choice as a value when the inappropriate exercise of choice may lead to the denial of a high school diploma and a lifetime of restricted opportunities for that same student. In our most prestigious private schools, students follow a rigorous curriculum that is largely prescribed. The opportunity to meet standards is directly linked to the curriculum and assessments of the schools. Failure, in other words, is less of an option when one cannot make choices associated with failure. How does curriculum choice relate to accountability? A holistic accountability system must identify not only the existence of a curriculum linked to standards but must also identify the extent to which students have the opportunity, indeed the obligation, to pursue that curriculum.

Teaching Strategies and Professional Practice

In addition to a consideration of student achievement, standards, and curriculum, a holistic accountability system must also consider teaching strategies and professional practices. Although it is a commonly held notion that teaching is an art rather than a science, a number of specific practices can be described, identified, and measured that are associated with superior student performance. It is equally true that the practice of medicine includes an element of art, but few patients would be satisfied with the notion that objective science plays less than a dominant role in the evaluation of the quality of a physician. So it is with education. Although we can honor the impact of the ineffable qualities of love, encouragement, and care for students, this acknowledgment of some undefined qualities does not diminish the importance of objectively identifiable professional practices that are associated with superior student performance.

We know, for example, that when students write more frequently, their ability to think, reason, analyze, communicate, and perform on tests will improve. Thus it is reasonable for policymakers to measure of the frequency with which students are required to write in class. Moreover, we can distinguish between student writing that is aimless and unfocused, such as the self-absorbed scatological reflections of teenagers in their journals, and the coherent and practiced expression that results when students are able to support an idea with details or persuade an audience with evidence. Other teaching strategies, such as the effective use of preassessment, continuous use of questions, and frequent changes in classroom practice based on a continuous stream of information from students, are all measurable and objective elements of effective professional practice.

Accountability for Leaders and Policymakers

A holistic accountability system will also include the impact of leadership and policy. The Achilles heel of most accountability systems is the exclusive focus on students and teachers as the objects of accountability. In fact, leaders and policymakers must bear equal scrutiny in an effective accountability system. For example, the common practice in which teaching resources are allocated based on seniority leads to the systematic misallocation of teacher quality away from schools with high populations of poor students to those schools with higher populations of economically advantaged students. When students of color and poverty are significantly less likely to have subject-matter-certified teachers than students who are economically advantaged (Archer, 1999; Haycock, 1998; Ingersoll, 1999), then this is a leadership and policy issue. Leaders and policymakers would never be allowed to allocate financial resources in the arbitrary and discriminatory manner in which they routinely allocate teaching resources. An effective accountability system calls leaders and policymakers to account for the pernicious decisions that they make and the discriminatory policies that they tolerate, no matter how time-honored those practices may be. More important, stakeholders in educational systems will be able to determine whether the causes of low student achievement lie with students and their families, or with the leadership and policy decisions that systematically give poor schools teachers with less experience, lower levels of certification, and fewer qualifications than are possessed by teachers assigned to wealthier schools. Without a consideration of these issues of teacher quality, it is easy to make misleading correlations between the income of students and their academic achievement.

Information and Evidence in a Holistic Accountability System

An effective accountability system requires evidence. Researchers create a false dichotomy when we break the world into quantitative and qualitative evidence, as if the existence of one precluded the utility of the other. In fact, a combination of quantitative and qualitative evidence is necessary for effective and holistic accountability. Measurement is important and it can provide valuable insights about proficiency, progress, and student success. Moreover, measurement lends an air of objectivity to the accountability process. The public is accustomed to measurement in everything from sporting contests to the business pages of the newspaper. It is interesting to note, however, that both the sports and business pages of the newspaper routinely include qualitative as well as quantitative information. In other words, we rarely report a box score without the story behind the numbers. We rarely see an earnings report in business without some elaboration of the antecedents of the profits or losses reported by the company. In most public and private endeavors, the general public understands the need for a balance of quantitative and qualitative information.

In the context of education, quantitative information includes test scores, percentages of students on free and reduced lunch, and objectively measurable elements of teaching strategies, leadership, and policy decisions in relation to standards, curriculum, and assessment. Qualitative information can provide a lens through which we better understand the numbers. By describing the context in which quantitative information is measured and reported, a holistic accountability report allows leaders and policymakers to understand when there is a genuine difference between two schools, and when there is merely a "distinction without a difference." Policy analysis depends on the identification of meaningful differences in effects and accurate identification of causes, and a combination of different types of evidence is the best mechanism to achieve such accurate and constructive analysis.

We begin with the premise that the purpose of accountability is the improvement of student achievement. If we accept this as the foundation for effective accountability, then we have no alternative except to pursue a course that will take us beyond the superficiality of test scores and reporting of variables that are most easily measured. If our objective is the understanding and improvement of student achievement, then we must identify the antecedents of excellence, including teaching and professional practices, leadership and policy decisions, standards and curriculum, and a host of other variables. The holistic accountability system described in this book creates a vision for how we can move beyond the rating, ranking, sorting, and evaluation that characterize the accountability debate today. By making accountability a constructive force for the improvement of education rather than a destructive force, we can elevate the discussion of educational reform ideas, illuminate these discussions with evidence, and reject the fact-free debate that so frequently characterizes discussions of educational policy.

CHAPTER 2

Caught in the Middle
The Consequences of Accountability

This chapter examines the consequences of accountability for students, teachers, and school leaders. Many popular notions of educational accountability tend toward one of two extremes. At one end of the argumentative continuum are those who pose this rhetorical question:

> Who could be against something as American and wholesome as accountability? Surely the only opponents would be those who fear accountability, and it is their fear that justifies ever more strict accountability systems. After all, teachers and administrators would only fear accountability if they have something to hide, so we had better make sure that we get all the dirty linen displayed and find out just how bad the educational system really is. And if the students, teachers, and administrators don't shape up, there will be severe penalties. That ought to get their attention!

The caricature at the other end of the continuum is that of the saintly public servant, chronically overworked, underpaid, and disrespected, working with children who never had a chance in a system designed to exploit the weak and powerless:

> Sure, go ahead and hold us accountable. All that you will prove is that schools with poor and minority kids underperform those schools that are full of kids who are rich and white. Then, to make matters worse, you will use the accountability system to take money away from the poor schools and give it to the rich schools. To top it all off, you will base these decisions on tests that everybody knows are racist, unreliable, and invalid. What you can't seem to understand is that the only people who can really evaluate schools are those inside them, the people who work in the trenches and understand what teachers and students must endure on a daily basis.

Both extremes shed more heat than light on the debate about educational accountability. First, we consider the myths surrounding the consequences of accountability, and then we examine the consequences for students, teachers, and school leaders. There is the potential for grave misuse of accountability; there is also the potential for the absence of accountability to have consequences that are equally unhelpful. The resolution of the two views is neither an accountability system that is draconian in its consequences nor one that is entirely benign. Only an accountability system that provides constructive and meaningful information to teachers, students, parents, and leaders can help the two factions agree on the issue. To have value, this information must be relevant to the decisions at hand and must be provided in a sufficiently timely manner so that it can have an impact on student achievement.

Accountability Myths

Myth #1: The Value of Consequences

Traditional adherents to behavioral psychology operate under the presumption that the fundamental human equation is one of rewards and punishments. Without such motivations, we wander aimlessly in search of gratification while assiduously avoiding pain. This logic has its limits not only with those who alternately administer food and electrical shocks to rats in a maze but also to those who seek to motivate human beings in educational systems. Thus the first myth that must be considered is the myth of the value of consequences.

If the theory of the value of consequences were true in the context of educational accountability, then those systems with the harshest punishments for poor performance should have the highest performance. Those states that impose sanctions including the loss of funds, denial of accreditation, closing of schools, and termination of employment for teachers and administrators should, under this theory, have the best educational results. Moreover, one would expect the success of punishments as effective motivators to be widely published. In fact, the record is quite inconsistent. States with punitive accountability systems have both high and low student achievement; states without punitive systems have high and low achievement. The evidence does not support the supposition that institutions respond well to the threat of punishment, nor is it clear that the absence of such a threat prevents strong and improving educational achievement. The myth of the value of consequences can thus be exposed for what it is: a hypothesis based on folklore rather than fact. The evidence reveals that students in states with the most severe consequences fail to outperform their counterparts who operated in the absence of such threats (Bracey, 2000).

The acceptance of the myth of the value of consequences rests on the belief that school leaders and educators are inherently malicious, seeking to do harm and actively avoiding good results for students. Only unwillingly and as the result of coercion will these malefactors change their ways and, under threat of state-imposed punishment, provide good educational practices for children. The same behaviorist approach applies to children, with adolescents doomed to their preferred state of ignorance were it not for the threat of the denial of a high school diploma as the inevitable consequence of the teenager's failure to perform adequately on a specific test. This is hardly news to researchers of the behavior of humans and institutions. Whether the consequence is a low grade (Guskey & Bailey, 2000) or the loss of accreditation and licensing, threats and intimidation are ineffective ways to motivate people and systems. It turns out that information, not threats, is the key to improving human performance. That information must contain feedback that is timely and relevant, not merely a recitation of failings and the award of an opaque score. There is, nonetheless, widespread popular support for the proposition that students should fail high school unless they perform adequately on a high stakes examination, with between 80% and 95% of Americans supporting such a policy, depending on the poll one wishes to believe (Sandowski, 2000).

Even the use of positive consequences has limits, as the state of California found. After a much-heralded attempt to use monetary incentives to improve student proficiency, the state discovered, to its chagrin, that many more schools performed at a higher-than-expected level. Thus, with a limited budget for rewards, the state retroactively reduced the amount sent to each school. Florida experienced similar perplexities with their attempted reward system, leaving more confusion than motivation as a result of the rewards (Sandham, 2000). When rewards and punishments are mysterious, late, unrelated to personal action, and subject to retroactive change, they are unlikely to influence the performance of students or adults.

The myth of the value of consequences has a deeper flaw than ineffectiveness and inaccuracy. The fundamental flaw is that it depends on malevolence rather than on goodwill. If the participants in the system are primarily motivated by money and the entrepreneurial rewards of higher performance, they will rarely be working in public education at all. If the participants in the system are primarily motivated by security, they will rarely be working in schools that are challenging, underperforming, and in need of heroic efforts for small improvements. If, on the other hand, the participants are motivated by the personal and professional satisfaction that is associated with student success, then they need an accountability system that will provide information that helps breed success. They need strategies, insights, and analysis far more than they need threats and consequences.

Myth #2: The Value of Freedom From Consequences

The second myth surrounding educational accountability is almost as dangerous as the first, and that is the myth that freedom from consequences is of ultimate value. In the first myth, teachers and leaders are lazy and malevolent leeches; in the second myth, teachers and leaders are heroic loners, possessing unique insight into their contributions to student learning. No external information can match their cosmic understanding of student achievement, and thus any accountability system is without value. Under the battle cry "Just leave me alone and let me teach!" the advocates of the second myth are convinced that the only good evaluation is self-evaluation (Ohanian, 1999).

Although this myth may appear to be a caricature, it has gained popular currency as a growing number of teachers, parents, and school leaders join in protests against accountability. In Spring 2001, parents in the high-income suburb of Scarsdale, New York were engaged in a coordinated effort to withdraw their children from school on test day. These parents were joined by their counterparts from Massachusetts to California, all of whom appeared to be convinced that accountability and testing would restrict teaching creativity and thus harm the education of students. The implication of their argument is that, without the influence of accountability and testing, children and their teachers would find reading, writing, and mathematics inconvenient intrusions into their day.

The real absurdity of the freedom myth is the underlying belief that only a regimen of test drills yields higher test scores and thus a classroom dominated by creativity, analysis, and rigor will produce students unable to perform well on tests. In repeated studies across the nation, I have found an exceptionally high relationship between the frequency of student writing, editing, and rewriting—perhaps the most time-consuming and demanding assignment for both students and teachers—and higher scores on multiple-choice tests in mathematics, science, and social studies (Reeves, 2000c). Contrary to the prevailing myth, it is not mindless test drills in a classroom devoid of creativity that lead to higher test scores. Rather, a classroom characterized by creative energy, challenge, and clear communication is the setting most likely to provide an intellectually rich environment and to develop students who are competent test takers. Not too many decades ago, we called this "good teaching" and did not need either tests or protests to encourage us to think, read, reflect, analyze, and write.

Resolving the Dilemma: A Holistic Approach

Holistic accountability has value not because it imposes sanctions or offers rewards but because it provides information that can be used by teachers, leaders, students, parents, and policymakers to improve student achievement. Holistic accountability assumes that the participants in the system are largely volunteers. Employees can find other work; students can mentally check out even when they are subject to compulsory attendance laws. The recognition that people are inherently volunteers in virtually any human system forces us to change the motivational strategy from consequences to the provision of information that is relevant and timely and that can be used appropriately.

Holistic accountability embraces the question "What's in it for me?" Such a question is not selfish but logical. Before any test is given, any measurement taken, or any description completed in a holistic system, the question must arise, "Can the stakeholders use this information productively?" In this way, holistic accountability systems go far beyond the superficial debate over whether students are "overtested" and asks the more relevant question, "How is testing information used to improve student achievement?" The answer to such a question may reveal that students are, indeed, overtested but are underassessed. Thus a holistic system often results in more measurements of student achievement over a greater span of time. This does not satisfy those who seek only to reduce the number of minutes that students spend taking tests, but it does address the concerns of those who demand that every moment of test taking is devoted to the production of information that is relevant and timely for making improved decisions for teaching, curriculum, leadership, and resource allocation.

Consequences for Students

The consequences for students in most educational accountability systems are widespread and serious. Consequences of accountability strike at the heart of the differences between holistic accountability and destructive accountability. In traditional systems, accountability is "done to" students and teachers. In holistic accountability systems, there are surely consequences, but a large body of evidence—never a single variable—is the rationale for action taken to improve teaching and learning. Of all of the consequences of accountability systems, surely the one with the most serious consequences for students are those that relate to promotion to the next grade and mandatory retention in the same grade.

By far the most common consequence of present methods of accountability is the denial of promotion based on student performance on a state-designated test. In some states, students must be proficient readers to advance to the 4th grade. In a growing number of states—26 at this writing (Coleman, 2000; Sandowski, 2000)—students must pass a high school graduation exam in order to qualify for a high school diploma. A closer examination of the consequences of these systems reveals that more is at stake than the presence or absence of a diploma or the decision to proceed to the next grade. The most dramatic consequence of accountability is what happens as a result of the decisions of students, teachers, parents, and school administrators to avoid these consequences.

First, we should acknowledge the potential for positive consequences. If a student is not reading in the 2nd or 3rd grade and the presence of an accountability system provides the impetus for that student to receive additional instruction and serious help in learning to read, then few people would question the salutary nature of such a consequence. If a student is unable to add, subtract, multiply, and divide in a high school algebra class and appears to be headed for failure and all its attendant consequences, then the consequence of a guided curriculum with additional support from caring adults can be a positive, even life-saving experience for the child.

Unfortunately, such positive consequences appear to be the exception rather than the rule. The most common consequence of failure is repetition of a grade or mandatory summer school. Neither strategy has a distinguished track record of effectiveness. In the nation's most closely watched and widely heralded experiment, the Chicago Public Schools require mandatory retention and summer schools for students who fail to meet the required score on a standardized test. The results are, at best, ambiguous. The most recent evidence suggests that although average test scores have increased, a significant portion of that increase may be due to the absence of students who dropped out rather than continued in the school system. We would hardly regard a medical experiment as successful if data were only taken from those who survived the experimental treatment, ignoring information from the patients who died. Only if information from students who drop out of school is included in an analysis of scores can the impact of mandatory retention programs be properly evaluated.

The Chicago experience is hardly unique, and a few districts have attempted to replace the club of retention with the carrot of multiple opportunities for student success (Janey, 2000). The most effective programs provide incentives for students to remain in school rather than drop out. The measures of success for these programs are counterintuitive. Rather than regard remediation as a negative reflection on the school, effective accountability systems include the identification of students in need and the provision of appropriate interventions for those students as a positive indicator.

Accountability systems also have an impact on the college and postsecondary opportunities for students. In Michigan, for example, more than 20% of parents withdrew their children from the Michigan Educational Assessment Program (MEAP) because they feared that a potentially negative score would adversely affect the college admissions opportunities for their children (Durbin, 1999). Ironically, it was the most economically advantaged and highest-performing students who withdrew from the test, leaving those schools with significantly lower average test scores than would have otherwise been the case. Some states are requiring actual college admissions tests, such as the American College Test (ACT) or SAT. Ironically, a growing number of competitive colleges are making these tests optional in their admissions programs, leaving students who wish to use their leadership, service, and academic experiences as the basis for admission lumped with those who rely principally on test scores.

Consequences for Teachers

The consequences of educational accountability for students are inseparable from the consequences for their teachers. If teachers perceive that they are penalized for working with the most challenging students because the test scores of students will be used to reflect the quality of the teacher, then experienced and highly qualified teachers have an automatic incentive to migrate from poor schools to those with students who have more economic and educational advantages. The Education Trust, among many other research institutions, has documented how students in poor urban schools receive more poor-quality instruction than their white and suburban counterparts (Johnston & Viadero, 2000). The natural consequence of the migration of the most qualified teachers from poor to rich schools is the disproportionate use of new teachers in the poorest schools. According to 60% of new public school teachers, most of them take over classrooms with insufficient experience, and 56% say their preparatory programs emphasized education theory at the expense of practical classroom challenges. School administrators confirmed these perceptions, with 44% of the administrators saying that new teachers did not have skills to maintain orderly classrooms and 68% laying the fault at the door of inadequate preparation programs (Henry, 2000). It is little wonder, then, that students in poor and urban schools not only work in an environment less conducive to effective learning but also take fewer challenging courses. Although the common temptation is to blame the indolence of the students, the more likely cause is the inadequate preparation of the teachers in those schools. The documentation of these generalities does not diminish the importance of the exceptions. There are, of course, wonderful teachers and successful students in high-poverty schools, just as there are unprofessional educators and poor students in wealthy schools. Acknowledging these exceptions, however, must not obscure the view of leaders and policymakers from the fundamental truth that the vast majority of school systems allocate teachers in a manner that results in inequitable educational opportunities for poor students.

Does this imply that administrators should simply reassign teachers from rich schools to poor schools and create "instant equity?" This approach was attempted in New York City in 2000, and the resignation of more than 1,700 teachers quickly followed. This left the poor schools not only with unqualified teachers but also without any teachers in some core curriculum areas. A more constructive approach has been taken in the Boston Public Schools, where significant economic and noneconomic incentives have been used to gain the voluntary acceptance of assignments to the most challenging schools by the most qualified and experienced teachers.

In addition to the direct impact on teachers, accountability systems have a significant indirect impact on teaching through the manner in which accountability systems influence curriculum design. The evidence is unambiguous—greater rigor in school curriculum is associated with greater levels of student success. Nevertheless, the vast majority of high school graduation tests are oriented toward the assessment of minimum basic skills in arithmetic and reading, and therefore, many schools have directed large parts of their curriculum to helping students achieve those skills. Ironically, this can result in increasing test scores at the same time that the quality and rigor of the curriculum is reduced.

Although popular mythology has it that accountability will lead to the discontinuation of the proverbial class in underwater basket weaving, it is far more likely that the teachers who had been teaching statistics, calculus, and trigonometry may have some of their time diverted to teaching a basic math skills class so that the number of students who can pass the high school graduation examination will increase. This need not be the case. In some exceptional schools, elective departments are taking up the challenge of helping students meet high school graduation requirements. At Ben Davis High School in Indianapolis, for example, the technology educators have revamped their curriculum to help students meet the requirements of the Indiana High School Graduation Examination. These creative educators changed the thinking of students who might have said "I don't have time to take a technology class because I have to get ready for the high school graduation exam" to "I had better take those technology classes because I have to get ready for the high school graduation exam." Because students reinforced their skills in technical reading and writing in the context of a technology course, they could pursue their interest in technology without sacrificing their development of essential skills.

Perhaps the single area in which accountability systems can have the most beneficial impact on teachers is the application to professional development programs. As undistinguished as undergraduate education programs may be in the eyes of the public, they are paragons of rigor and relevance compared to many staff development programs that are vacuous wastes of time and money. Because professional development courses have operated on the standard of popularity rather than effectiveness, they have rarely been exposed to any systematic evaluation of effectiveness. When, however, these programs are included in an accountability program in which policymakers, school leaders, and teachers can systematically observe the relationship—or lack of it—between staff development programs and student achievement, then more than a few of these insipid wastes of time will be on the chopping block. Guskey (2000) has created the most systematic approach that links professional development to comprehensive accountability.

Consequences for Administrators

The national teacher shortage that is looming in the early years of the 21st century will soon be matched by a serious shortage of administrators. It is common practice for school superintendents to insist on a multiyear contract because they fear that changes in board politics, totally beyond the control of the incumbent superintendent, can adversely affect the future employment of the district leader. One can safely predict that this trend will soon extend to principals and other school leaders who are implored to take the reins of a deeply troubled school. Rather than see their career in tatters because of their association with a "failed" school or, worse yet, have their professional credentials threatened by a state accountability system, school leaders will become entrepreneurial free agents, demanding and receiving multiyear contracts and protection of their salaries, if not guarantees of their jobs.

For those few administrators who gain a reputation as turnaround artists, there will be agents representing them just as professional consulting firms now routinely represent prospective superintendents in negotiations with the board. The notion of a standard administrative pay scale will become obsolete, and districts must then compete for the talents of the most effective school leaders. Even the most entrepreneurial school leaders, however, will be hard-pressed to create qualified teachers from the pool of people with emergency credentials, limited experience, and limited subject-matter knowledge. Only when they have the flexibility to offer incentives for experienced and qualified teachers will school leaders be able to transform failing schools into successful ones. The flip side of being able to hire and retain the most effective faculty members will be the ability of school leaders to dismiss the least effective faculty members. Both of these powers are remote fantasies in most school systems. Until such fundamental structural reforms are in place, administrators are left with the fantasy of association: Those in the vicinity of success are successful, whereas those in close proximity to failures must be the cause. Little wonder, then, that the vast majority of administrators, including those who are talented and successful leaders, will have little incentive to become associated with the most deeply troubled schools.

Impact on Community Leaders and Policymakers

Accountability information can have important implications for leaders and policymakers, particularly when the variables that are gathered lead to pre-ordained conclusions. Consider one of the most frequent reforms now under way in more than 20 states: mandatory class size reduction. The federal commitment to class size reduction exceeds $1.2 billion, and states have committed many times that amount to reduce the ratio of students to teachers (Johnston & Viadero, 2000). Unfortunately, class size alone is rarely an adequate solution to the complex challenge of student achievement. In the nation's largest scale and most expensive experiment, California has committed billions of dollars to ensure that no more than 20 students are present in the early elementary grade classrooms. Unfortunately, the emphasis on quantity rather than quality has led to a situation in which the poorest districts have no more than 20 students to 1 unqualified teacher who has no teaching certificate and little or no professional background for the position. The rest of the story will be predictable: Student achievement will not improve and someone will allege that class size reduction didn't work after all, so the funding for the initiative should be diverted elsewhere. In fact, a careful analysis of the class size research would have revealed that quality was more important than quantity (Henry, 2000), something most class size researchers have acknowledged.

Despite these pitfalls, there are opportunities for accountability to open the door to more constructive approaches for community leaders and policymakers. Such a constructive approach begins with the mission and values of our schools. If the decisions of leadership and policy-making bodies are based on the twin goals of excellence and equity, then accountability systems will be more than a superficial scorecard. On the contrary, accountability systems can be dynamic tools that provide relevant and meaningful information for the improvement of student achievement and the maintenance of equity for all stakeholders in the system.

One of the most significant areas in which policymakers can have a positive influence on educational accountability systems is the creation of central office accountability. Rather than the traditional notion in which accountability is the exclusive burden of students and teachers, a holistic approach to accountability requires that every leader in the central office also bears a direct and significant responsibility for the achievement of the district goals. Thus the central office can measure and monitor the extent to which a large pool of qualified teaching and administrative candidates is available for every vacancy. The central office can also measure and monitor the extent to which risks are avoided, costs are reduced, and risk is minimized so that more resources are available for student learning.

The creation of a centralized accountability system creates an important clarification of a conundrum that plagues many school systems: the tension between decision making by the central office and the ambiguity of site-based decision making. The architecture of this system (see Chapter 7) makes clear that there are common, systemwide, nonnegotiable goals. In other words, site-based decision making is used to determine how, not whether, to achieve the goals of equity and excellence in the system. Without such clear differentiation of school-based accountability from central office-based accountability, the vacuum is filled with ambiguity, tension, and uncertainty.

Conclusion

The consequences of accountability need not be negative. Unfortunately, most of the consequences currently associated with state accountability systems have been less than helpful for students, teachers, and administrators. Students avoid the wasteland of retention through the pursuit of low-level skills. Teachers and administrators avoid the guilt by association with failing schools by using their experience and seniority to move as far away as possible from those schools, leaving them in the hands of less capable and experienced colleagues. Policymakers add kerosene to the inferno by creating perverse incentives for everyone involved, leaving few good deeds unpunished. The vision of holistic accountability can reverse this insanity, with appropriate incentives for teachers and administrators, assistance rather than punishment for students, and equity in the application of accountability consequences that include standards of performance for every member of the system, from board members to senior administrators to the central office to schools.

CHAPTER 3

A Better Way
Using Holistic Accountability to Improve Teaching and Learning

T his chapter describes an alternative to traditional educational accountability in which the primary aim is the ranking, sorting, and labeling of
schools, teachers, and school districts. Holistic accountability is neither an
isolated report nor a series of tests but, rather, a continuous cycle in which research informs professional practice and professional practice yields evidence of its impact on student achievement. Based on this evidence, leaders
and policymakers can make informed decisions and rationally allocate resources. These resources, in turn, support more effective research, professional practice, and leadership, as illustrated in Figure 3.1.

Research Informs Practice

In the first part of the holistic accountability cycle, data are gathered on both
student achievement and the underlying causes of student achievement. Unlike most traditional accountability systems that rely exclusively on student
achievement data alone, holistic accountability systems examine and measure the "antecedents of excellence," including teaching practices, curriculum, technology, parental involvement, and a host of other indicators that
practitioners believe are related to student achievement. Rather than presume that various programs are effective as a result of their good intentions,
holistic accountability systems test such underlying assumptions. If, for example, technology applications are believed to support improved student
achievement, then the accountability system should find a correlation between the use of technology in the classroom and improvements in student
achievement. If there is no such correlation, then one of two things is possible.
Either the technology applications do not have the positive impact that its

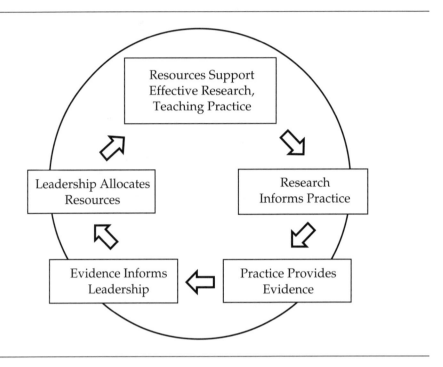

Figure 3.1. The Holistic Accountability Cycle: Using Accountability to Improve Teaching and Learning

advocates had hoped, or the manner in which technology applications are being measured is inadequate. In either case, leaders and policymakers have learned something quite valuable.

In some cases, the accountability system will reveal weaknesses in programs and resources can then be diverted to more productive and effective programs. In other cases, the accountability system itself will be improved because the measurements of program implementation can be refined. In the instances of technology applications, for example, it is entirely possible that schools are measuring the wrong thing when they boast of the "number of wired classrooms" or the "number of Internet connections" or even the "number of Web site searches" by students and teachers. A holistic accountability system might lead to a change in the measurement from an abstract counting of connections to a more meaningful and specific measurement of how technology is used in teaching and learning. For example, middle school science teachers could identify the percentage of their classroom assessments that directly incorporate technology for word processing, analysis of data, and the creation of graphs. The results of students in the classes that exhibit a large quantity of such assessments can be compared with the results of students in classes where no such technology integration has occurred. Such a comparison will never be the final word on the utility of technology in the classroom, but it is a start to more informed decision making that is based on evidence rather than supposition.

In those cases where technology investments appear to be unrelated to student achievement, analysts and school leaders should consider whether the number of computer connections (and their attendant costs) increased substantially but the amount of student writing, problem solving, and research-ing remained stagnant. If student work, thinking, and practice did not materi-ally change as a result of the mere installation of technology, then we should not be surprised. The same situation would be the result if school officials re-placed a #2 pencil with a mechanical pencil, maintained the identical curricu-lum and student activities, counted the number of mechanical pencils in use, and then were bewildered that student achievement did not increase as the number of mechanical pencils in use had increased.

When research informs practice, then school leaders, teachers, and policymakers get relevant information in a timely manner on the most impor-tant indicators of student achievement. They receive much more than a set of test scores; they gain insight into the antecedents of excellence. This leads to the next part of the holistic accountability cycle, evidence from effective practice.

Practice Provides Evidence

The most common evidence in accountability systems is the test score as a measurement of student achievement. Sometimes, the public views the per-centile rank; other times, they see average test scores; and in other cases, they receive a somewhat more relevant statistic, such as the percentage of students who are proficient or better according to the state standards. But no matter what statistic is used, no matter how elegant the mathematics or how careful the calculations, those who provide only test scores never shed meaningful light on the teaching, learning, curriculum, leadership, and policymaking that were associated with those scores. In sporting contests, we routinely consider not only the score but also the actions of the players and coaches that led to the final score. In medicine, we consider not only a judgment regarding the health of the patient but what the patient and doctor did or failed to do to achieve the present state of health. In the lists of test scores from traditional accountability systems, the missing link is evidence of what happened before the score was calculated. In brief, we need not just results but also evidence of the causes associated with those results. We need to measure, understand, and report the professional practices, leadership decisions, policy options, and curriculum choices that were associated with the test scores.

Professional practices of educators are seldom reported because of the folk wisdom that suggests that teaching, somewhat like medieval conceptions of medicine, is an indefinable art. Modern analyses have discounted such a simplistic and primitive view. Robert Marzano (2000; Marzano & Kendall, 1998) makes the point bluntly, using the statistical notion of "effect size" to draw an important analogy to the hard sciences. Effect size is, in plain terms, a measure of the impact of a treatment compared to a group that did not receive the treatment.[1] If there were multiple medical studies that analyzed treatments that had an effect size of .3, then it would be regarded as so dramatically important that researchers would stop the study and immediately seek to make such a treatment available to the general public. This "stop the study" standard is a reasonable benchmark for educational research. It implies neither perfection nor certainty but only a degree of confidence that would, in the medical context, be sufficient to stop the study and give the treatment to the public.

We can demystify the practice of teaching by measuring in clear and unambiguous terms such practices as the use of student-identified goals, teacher monitoring of progress, preassessment that influences instruction, the representation of knowledge in nonlinguistic forms, and the maintenance of a record of student knowledge, to name just a few techniques that are objectively observable and measurable. When teachers use these techniques, the bulk of research suggests that such professional practices are associated with improved achievement. In the context of holistic accountability, each school, district, and classroom can draw its own conclusions.

Systematic measurement itself creates an impact on the results. The well-known Pareto effect suggests that the mere act of study and observation will influence the results of an experiment for the better. It is thus no surprise that some popular educational innovations require 80% agreement by the faculty before a new program will be attempted. When an endorsement implies an intellectual bet on the success of a program, it is small wonder that such programs succeed. As in the cases of the Pareto effect, whether the factory lights are dimmed or brightly lit, the change and the belief in the change can work wonders on the motivation, efficiency, and effectiveness of the workers. Holistic accountability systems allow school leaders and policymakers to distinguish the merely popular from the genuinely effective. The essential question is not whether a particular instruction strategy is effective somewhere else, but rather whether it is effective *here*. Only a mechanism that systematically relates the implementation of an instructional, curriculum, leadership, or other technique to its impact on student achievement will establish itself as having crossed the threshold from popularity to effectiveness.

The subtle distinction between what is popular and what is effective leads us to a consideration of the next phase of the holistic accountability cycle, the use of evidence to inform leadership decisions.

Evidence Informs Leadership

Educational leaders and policymakers are besieged with requests for resources and attention. The catchphrase "research based" is associated with almost all these requests. Few, if any, such proposals, however, provide evidence of sustained effectiveness in the same environment in which the leaders are rendering the decision. In other words, a citation from a study that concludes that a reading program is effective in Topeka is only the beginning of persuasive policy research for school leaders in other districts. The use of a holistic accountability system provides the critical next step: the documentation that the reading program was not only effective in Topeka, but it was also effective in our own district.

Decision makers are confronted with too many requests for too few resources, and the catchphrase "research based" may suggest that all programs that have some research attached to them have equal value. When the research evidence stems from holistic accountability, there is a clear advantage in the form of multivariate analysis. This is not as daunting as it may sound. Perhaps the phrase "real world" would be an appropriate substitute for "multivariate," as both imply the same level of complexity. The real world is never comprised of the presence or absence of a single variable, such as a new class or book. Rather, the real world includes many variables, including not only variations among students but also variations in the curriculum and teaching strategies to which they are exposed. Only a simultaneous examination of all these variables yields some insight into the relative importance of the impact of each variable.

In college, "multivariate analysis" sounds impressive. But if the subject were baseball, even the student who avoided multivariate analysis like the plague would not hesitate to venture that "hitting is more important than pitching, particularly in those high-altitude ballparks," or that "defense wins championships in football, especially if the quarterback is fragile and throwing options are limited." In fact, we routinely recognize that human systems have many variables, and the superficial association of a single cause with a single effect offers little insight, whether the subject is weather, sports, or academic achievement. The very word "holistic" suggests a systems approach to accountability and thus is contrary to the labels, ranks, and bivariate inferences that are so frequently found in traditional educational accountability systems.

Although our search for easy answers is natural, the recognition of multiple variables is not elusive and the term multivariate should not obscure the application of common sense. As I write this chapter (already full of too many sports illustrations), my 7-year-old son just lost a basketball game. Our conversation after the game illustrates that multiple variables such as height, position, movement, and ball direction are within the grasp of a second grader. Jamie's team did not merely lose; it was hammered, and all the kids knew it. I asked, naively, "Jamie, what did you learn from the game?" He replied with the wisdom of a 7-year-old, "I learned that we lost." Only after considerable probing, hugging, consoling, and gentle questioning did we find that there were other lessons:

Jamie: He was shorter than me, but he got the ball away from me!

Me: Yes—what else did they do?

Jamie: Every time I tried to get the ball, they passed it to somebody else!

Me: So what do you think we should do next time?

Jamie: Go to where the ball is?

Me: But what if they pass it to another guy again?

Jamie: Maybe I should go to where the ball is going, not just where it is.

I think we're making progress. Jamie and I both understood that there are many different factors at work in a game, but it takes some reflection to identify and understand how each of those factors is related to success or failure.

If we expect evidence from many different variables, including student achievement, professional practices, curriculum, leadership, resources, demographic characteristics, and other data to influence leadership decisions in a rational manner, then it is imperative that multiple causes are recognized. Just as there is a logical minefield in the presumption of single causes and single effects, the postulation of multiple causes can lead policymakers and leaders to throw up their hands and exclaim, "The roots of the problem are so varied and complex, it doesn't seem to matter what we do!" That is where multivariate analysis provides some insights, for it helps teachers, leaders, and policymakers not only to recognize the existence of multiple causes but also to identify two common phenomena: covariation and confounding variables.

Covariation occurs when two factors behave in very similar ways, and thus one can easily mistake one apparent cause for the underlying real cause. Consider the following common example. A school system noted that the greater the percentage of students who were eligible for free and reduced lunch in a school, the lower the test scores. Using only these two variables, the relationship might look like the grid shown in Figure 3.2.

Believers in the bell curve might give willing assent to Figure 3.2. Were we to turn back the clock 80 years, the horizontal axis could be replaced by skin color. Let us be blunt: There are people who wear academic robes as well as those who wear white robes who sincerely believe that melanin content is inversely related to test scores. There is just one problem. Another variable, teaching certification and advanced training, is also negatively related to percentage of students in a school who are poor or members of minority ethnic

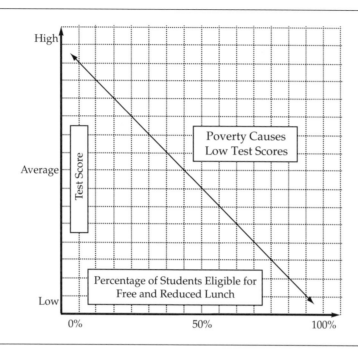

Figure 3.2. Free and Reduced Lunch Is Related to Test Scores

groups. Consider Figure 3.3, taken from an actual school district, in which the percentage of teachers with advanced degrees was correlated to demographic characteristics.

A comparison of Figures 3.2 and 3.3 makes clear that there is a substantial degree of covariation—a similar relationship to other variables—between student test performance and the percentage of teachers who have advanced degrees. It is not, it turns out, poverty or skin color that is the real causal variable but, rather, a "confounding variable"—teacher qualification—that is far more relevant in relation to student achievement. The observations of other researchers (Archer, 2000; Haycock et al., 1999; Ingersoll, 1999) make clear that the phenomenon observed in Figure 3.2 is hardly an isolated relationship. Throughout the nation, children of color and children who are poor are much less likely to have teachers who are certified in the subject matter that they teach or, for that matter, certified in any area. This is directly related to the holistic approach to accountability. Faced with only two variables, casual observers can easily blame parents, students, or unchangeable demographic characteristics. When confronted with a multivariate approach, policymakers must take more responsibility for those variables they can influence. Specifically, demographic characteristics are not nearly as subject to change as school system policies with regard to the equitable assignment of teachers. Board members and school leaders can influence those policies, and their

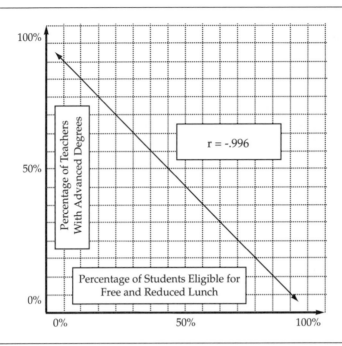

Figure 3.3. Poor Students Are Less Likely to Have Teachers With Advanced Degrees

decision making is a variable that is at least as powerful as demographic characteristics.

Leadership Allocates Resources

The next step in the holistic accountability cycle is the allocation of resources by educational leaders. Resource allocation decisions include not only money but also teaching quality, staff develxopment time, curriculum alternatives, technology, leadership focus, and a host of other limited resources that must be allocated with care. Every time leaders and policymakers are confronted with a request for limited resources, they establish priorities. Shall we reduce class size or buy more technology? Shall we raise salaries or improve building safety? Shall we improve teacher training or provide additional special education positions? Shall we require teachers to spend six hours in the presence of a motivational speaker or allow them to collaborate on the consistent and accurate scoring of student work? All too frequently, these decisions are made based on personal preferences rather than evidence, and at best, there is a nod toward the ideal of "data-driven decision making" or "research-based" policies. Rarely, however, does leadership have the ability to dig into its account-ability data and identify the specific relationship of their previous invest-ments in class size reduction, teacher training, technology, or many other resource allocation decisions to the impact on student performance. The rea-son for the scarcity of data-driven decisions is not the absence of will by edu-cational leaders but the failure of accountability systems to provide a continu-ous analysis of relationships between investments and results. What passes for research is the assertion of a salesman rather than a systematic examina-tion of the relationship between the application of specific and quantifiable teaching and leadership strategies (such as resource allocation) and specific and quantifiable student results. With a holistic accountability system, sys-tematic analysis replaces glib salesmanship.

Resource allocation decisions based on accountability data can yield sub-stantial benefits. Consider the controversial issue of class size. There is abun-dant research (Achilles, 1999) that appears to establish the obvious: Smaller class size is better than larger class size. Closer analysis of the evidence reveals that the relationship between smaller class size and student achievement is not linear. In other words, one can conclude that more than 37 students per class is a bad idea and, in general, fewer than 17 students per class is a good idea. This does not, however, necessarily prove that a classroom with 26 stu-dents will result in better achievement than a classroom with 28 students. Recognition of nonlinear relationships has important implications for lead-ers. Rather than investing millions of dollars in an across-the-board class size reduction, leaders might consider the multivariate nature of educational ac-countability. Should the same dollars be devoted to improved teacher quality and certification? Should the same dollars be devoted to targeted reduction to get particular classrooms from 28 students down to 17 students while leaving other classrooms at 28 or perhaps 30 students per class? Effective resource al-location decisions require a consideration of all the accountability data and necessitate holistic analysis.

Resources Support Effective Research, Teaching Practice, and Leadership

The final step in the accountability cycle is not final at all but, rather, the pen-ultimate step that leads to the repetition of the cycle. One of the most impor-tant resource allocation decisions that leaders can make is the support of ac-countability research, and the time for leaders to consider that information. Moreover, teachers need to have the time to consider accountability research.

It is not only the superintendent and board that use accountability data. Classroom teachers and principals who must individually examine their own data and the data from other schools and classrooms make some of the best uses of accountability data. These professionals must consider not only test scores but also the information on professional practices, leadership decisions, curriculum alternatives, and other information from a holistic accountability system. They can ask questions such as "How do schools that are similar to ours have high achievement? What practices did they use? What curriculum did they have? What leadership decisions did they make?" When accountability consists only of a litany of test scores, teachers will never have productive discussions of accountability data. Only when accountability information includes insights into how the professional practices and curriculum decisions of teachers and administrators affect student achievement will their discussions be productive and constructive.

Accountability: A Work in Progress

Here is the bad news: Educational accountability is never finished. Even the highest-performing schools can learn how to improve from the application of the holistic accountability cycle. Complacency is not an option. Here is the good news: No child, no teacher, no leader, no school should be labeled with last year's test scores. Even the lowest performing schools can gain insight into their strengths and how to leverage their best practices. Discouragement and resignation are not options. With holistic accountability, the process of continuous learning applies to leaders and teachers as surely as it applies to students. Leaders must, in brief, practice what they preach.

Note

1. This book is intended for a lay audience and thus excessive technical and statistical jargon has been avoided. For those who wish to explore the notion of effect size in educational research at greater length, Dr. Marzano's meta-analysis with a thorough discussion of effect size and its applicability to educational research can be found at www.mcrel.org.

CHAPTER 4

Community Collaboration
Making Accountability
a Constructive Force

N o school leader, however capable or intelligent, can create an effective accountability system alone. Any change effort, particularly one with the emotional associations that inevitably surround anything with the appellation "accountability," must be the result of a collaborative effort. This chapter describes the process for engaging an Accountability Task Force that will not only create a holistic accountability system, but will also monitor the implementation of the system. Such a collaborative approach steps back from the "Us versus Them" approach that so frequently characterizes relationships between administrators and teachers and, for that matter, between governing boards and administrators. The Task Force may be more cumbersome, and it is certainly slower, than a single person working alone. Nevertheless, the successful implementation of holistic accountability depends on the active involvement of many stakeholders.

Building Bridges: The Accountability Task Force

Developing a comprehensive accountability system is a labor-intensive process. The first step in undertaking this work is the establishment of an Accountability Task Force. The Task Force will have primary responsibility for coordination and oversight as the accountability system is developed and implemented. Because Task Force members will have a number of difficult, time-consuming responsibilities, it is important to make this clear to potential Task Force participants before they agree to join. Members should be willing to serve for a minimum of six 2-hour meetings during the design phase of their work, and then participate in quarterly meetings thereafter. Terms of service are typically two years.

The Task Force reports to the superintendent who, in turn, reports to the board. The political dynamics of some school systems are such that the Accountability Task Force reports directly to the board of education. In chartering the Accountability Task Force, the board must make these reporting relationships clear.

Beyond "The Usual Suspects"

Even in those instances where stakeholder involvement appears to be a matter of practice, the depth and breadth of that involvement may be less than ideal. Frequently, stakeholder involvement includes little more than committee meetings of the usual suspects: active parents, vocal teachers, veteran principals, community activists, and Chamber of Commerce members whose job description includes serving as a liaison to local governmental and educational institutions. Although each of those groups deserves representation, we should not accept as a demonstrated truth that the "usual suspects" are actually representative of the stakeholders in a community.

Active parents are essential for school systems, but many other parents feel disenfranchised and removed from meaningful influence in the schools. This group of parents may remain silent during school committee meetings; after all, they were not invited to the table. But they are not silent during bond issue elections, board elections, and initiatives to support or oppose diversion of public education resources.

Chamber of Commerce members may represent legitimate business interests, but it would serve school systems well to carefully analyze their business community. Where are the numbers? Where is the growth? Where is the employment of students and graduates? Are those enterprises represented only by the members of the Chamber of Commerce, or are those enterprises the thousands of small entrepreneurial businesses that have been the engine of the economic boom at the dawn of the 21st century? If so, then wise school leaders will cast a net throughout the community to ensure that Accountability Task Force members include traditionally underrepresented—but very important—stakeholder groups.

If a Task Force is to be inclusive, then it is imperative that the leadership of the district cast a wide net, including a diverse mix of stakeholders who hold in common a commitment to public education but whose differences can be striking. Retired persons, small business owners, single parents, and other unlikely and diverse stakeholders must be at your table. Start by making a list of the "usual suspects" for your Task Force, and then engage in some serious brainstorming to expand the list far beyond that initial list. After you have 30 or 40 names, then create the final list of 18 to 24 prospective Task Force mem-

---

Wednesday, August 15

Dear ____:

We would like to ask you to serve on the Accountability Task Force for the Green Valley School District. The purpose of the Task Force is to create an accountability system that will accomplish these objectives:

- Improve student achievement
- Communicate with students, parents, and the community
- Give our board of education reliable information about what educational initiatives are most effective in our community.

The Task Force will initially meet monthly, starting Friday, October 15th, and on the 2nd Friday of every month through April from noon through 2:00 p.m. in the district office at 201 Poplar Avenue. Lunch will be served. Please only accept this invitation if you are able to attend these meetings.

The Task Force will make its recommendations to the Board of Education at its May 21st meeting. After that meeting, the Task Force will continue to meet quarterly to analyze accountability information and to review the accountability reports provided to the board and community.

Only 18 people from our community will serve on this vitally important Task Force. We know that your time is valuable and hope that you will give serious consideration to this invitation. If you would like to discuss the duties and role of the Task Force, please call us at any time.

Sincerely,

Jane Cohen, Superintendent   Richard Sackett, President
Green Valley Schools   Board of Education

Figure 4.1. Sample Letter of Invitation

bers who will be invited to join the group. Only in this way can you achieve the balance, inclusiveness, and ultimate success of the Accountability Task Force.

Asking key members of community groups to serve on the Accountability Task Force sends a clear message: *We need you, but we also will be accountable to you and to the community.* A sample letter of invitation to join the Task Force appears in Figure 4.1.

Job Description for Accountability Task Force Members

Even if the letter of invitation is as clear as possible, some future members of the Accountability Task Force may feel as if they have received a cryptic invitation from the superintendent's secretary. They know the meeting is about "education" and perhaps are attracted to the notion of "accountability," but that's as far as it goes. Although there are risks in full disclosure of the challenges involved in membership in the Accountability Task Force, the rewards for the district are far greater. You may consider attaching a version of this description (Figure 4.2) to the letter of invitation.

You may choose to use a job description that is somewhat less intimidating, but you must clearly communicate your expectations to the prospective Accountability Task Force members. At the very least, the prospective members must know that you expect them to attend faithfully six meetings of 2 to 3 hours in duration. After the accountability system is approved by the board, the Task Force members will normally meet two or three times each year to review the research yielded by the accountability system and to review proposed changes to the system. In addition, members will be expected to read and think about some complex and difficult documents, ranging from test data to personnel evaluation forms. Finally, they will be expected to deal constructively with conflicting opinions and perspectives. If they find disagreement and strongly held opinions to be unpleasant or distasteful, then this is probably not the right Task Force for them.

Duties of the Accountability Task Force

Although the board of education should give the Accountability Task Force an explicit charter with clear duties, it may be helpful to begin the process with some common responsibilities that this group will undertake.

1. *Identify and describe the existing accountability system.* Every school system has an accountability system, whether or not it bears such a label. There are recognition and rewards systems, evaluation forms, achievement reports, and so on. The first duty of the Task Force is to identify the existing accountability systems. All the work of the Task Force can be undermined if they produce something labeled the "accountability plan" and later find out that the board and community have an alternative agenda—the real accountability system—that was beyond the purview of the Task Force. In the course of their review of the existing accountability system, the Task Force should review the following documents:

Purpose: The Task Force will develop a new educational accountability system for our schools, and review accountability data for reports to the superintendent and board.

Experience and Education Needed: Sincere interest in our community and the success of our schools is required. Technical background and educational backgrounds are not necessary. In fact, Task Force members *without* a technical background in education, testing, and statistics are particularly needed. These members will help the Task Force provide information that is clear to every citizen in the community.

Report to: Board of Education, through the superintendent of schools

Duration: During the first six months, the Task Force will meet monthly for two-hour meetings (please see the attached schedule). After that, the Task Force will meet quarterly for two-hour meetings. The term of membership is two years.

Responsibilities: Prior to each meeting, Task Force members will be expected to read materials distributed by the Task Force coordinator. During each meeting, members will be expected to participate actively in the deliberations of the Task Force. In order to continue membership on the Task Force, attendance at five of the six initial monthly meetings is necessary.

Figure 4.2. Job Description: Accountability Task Force Member

- Strategic plan
- Accreditation plan
- Building improvement plans
- Board goals and objectives
- Superintendent goals and objectives
- Teacher and administrator evaluation forms
- Bargaining agreements that govern teacher and administrator evaluation forms
- Research department publications on student achievement
- State and district "report cards" or other documents that evaluate school performance
- Independent evaluations, audits, and reports that have been conducted in the past three years.

2. *Define the principles that will govern the accountability system.* Too frequently, groups begin with accountability indicators and argue the merits of one particular test or another. The essential diversity of views of the Task Force

will lead inevitably to strong disagreements on such matters. Therefore, the mission of the Task Force is better served if the group focuses first on principles that bring them together. For example, teachers, administrators, parents, and business representatives should all be able to agree that principles such as fairness, equity, and accuracy should govern the system. Step 2 of Chapter 7 offers some additional suggestions for the principles that can govern an accountability system. Values and principles create opportunities for reasonable resolutions to disagreements over the details of an accountability system as well as a means to reassure all stakeholders that the Task Force is not engaging in a "gotcha!" exercise but, rather, is committed to an accountability plan that adheres to values held by all stakeholders.

3. *Identify* who *within and outside the school district is accountable.* If the only people held accountable are 4th graders and the only accountability mechanism is sending legions of 9-year-olds to summer school, then the deliberations of the Task Force should not be particularly taxing. If, on the other hand, accountability includes not only students but teachers, administrators, board members, and the community at large, then a completely different set of accountability indicators will follow.

4. *Identify qualitative and quantitative indicators for performance by students, teachers, and leaders.* Just because something can be measured does not automatically qualify it for inclusion in an accountability system. Accountability is far more than a recitation of test scores. The Task Force will inevitably face two challenges. First, Task Force members will be overwhelmed with data. Despite the apparent abundance of information, they may conclude that some data can be interesting without meeting the requirements for a fair, effective, and comprehensive system. Second, the Task Force may find that, despite the overwhelming amount of data (typically test scores) that are available, important pieces to the accountability puzzle are missing. Most school systems fail to measure critical educational practices and results, including classroom-level assessment and teaching practice. These historical omissions should not lead to their exclusion from the accountability system but, rather, create a challenge for the Task Force to identify new information that must be gathered at the same time they are identifying some time-honored elements of test reports that may no longer play a meaningful role in the accountability system. Thus the Task Force must consider the data presently available as well as the information that may be important but that has not traditionally been gathered by the school system.

Reality now intrudes into theory. Few teachers document and quantify their practices. Few principals document and quantify their leadership strategies. Thus we are left with the classical research error in which the investigator measures those things easiest to measure rather than those things that are most important. This explains the fixation of educational researchers on the easily measured quantities of skin color, gender, and economics and the studied avoidance of the more challenging measurement problems of teaching and leadership strategies. The past, fortunately, is not prologue. Holistic accountability demands that we elevate importance and relevance over accessibility and ease. Chapter 7 provides specific advice on how to measure the most important variables in your accountability system.

5. *Determine the architecture of the accountability system.* Once indicators have been identified, how do they fit into a system? Will every piece of available information be reported on every school? Will schools have some choice with regard to the indicators that they use?

6. *Create an accountability communication system.* Typical accountability systems offer an annual "report card" to the community. Because the amount of information is typically overwhelming, there is inevitable disappointment when the media oversimplifies the process. An effective accountability communication system may well include an annual report, but it will also include information throughout the year. Moreover, because the primary purpose of the accountability system is the improvement of student achievement, reports are not only made in the form of voluminous documents and formal board presentations but in a series of very brief summaries for a variety of audiences. These audiences include individual students and parents, who can see how their efforts contribute to the accountability system. Other key audiences for accountability reports throughout the year include teachers, principals, and central office administrators, all of whom must be able to use that information to make midcourse corrections and improve their own professional practice in pursuit of the goals of the system. In other words, communication about accountability is not merely an exercise in public relations; communication provides essential feedback to the stakeholders in the system so that they can improve.

Coordinating and Communicating With the Task Force

A senior administrative officer of the school district or an independent facilitator should have primary responsibility for coordinating Task Force affairs and communicating with Task Force members. Effective communication for the Accountability Task Force has the following characteristics:

- **Advance Notice and Time for Reflection:** Agendas and supporting documents are always distributed at least 10 days in advance. It is not reasonable to expect Task Force members to read complex documents during a meeting or to respond to alternative ideas on accountability systems without first taking time to reflect on those ideas. Administrators and Task Force members who attempt to distribute written materials during a meeting should be gently but firmly reminded of the group procedure that all materials must be distributed in advance in order for those items to be considered by the Task Force. Without such advance distribution, the matter can wait until the next Task Force meeting.

- **Documentation and History:** Every Task Force member should have a large three-ring notebook into which all documents and various drafts of the accountability plan are placed. Subtle changes in wording can have significant implications for the accountability system, and the memory of Task Force members is a poor substitute for careful and complete documentation of deliberations and changes.

- **Deliberation Between Meetings:** With the availability of computer e-mail lists, it is easy—indeed, necessary—for a constant flow of thought and deliberation to take place between meetings. The problem with most Task Forces and committees is that such between-meeting deliberation is typically limited to a few people who happen to cross paths. It is far more constructive (and less divisive) if these between-meeting deliberations occur openly. Unlike an e-mail exchanged between two people, an e-mail list can allow a single e-mail address to reach every member of the Task Force. Even if a deliberation begins as a conversation between two Task Force members, the use of the e-mail list allows every member of the Task Force to follow the thread of the conversation and add their own perspective and contribution to the deliberation. For Task Force members without access to the Internet, the Task Force coordinator should compile paper copies of the electronic memoranda and distribute them to Task Force members at least every two weeks. Task Force members without a computer can then submit their contributions to the discussion through the coordinator who, in turn, will post those comments to the e-mail list.

- **Communication Outside the Task Force:** An imperative for the Task Force is the agreement of members that the deliberations—particularly drafts and trial balloons—are not presented as settled policy or Task Force decisions until they have been approved by the superintendent and board. The Task Force is a deliberative body created for the purpose of making recommendations. It is not a policy-making body, and none of the members should labor under such an illusion. It is particularly inappropriate for Task Force members to talk about their deliberations to the media. That is the job of the superintendent, *not* Task Force members.

Building Consensus:
The Limits of "Rules of Procedure"

During the first meeting, the Task Force must establish its norms and proce-dures. Examples of issues to be addressed could include the following:

- Facilitator and/or chairperson (unless the superintendent has already identified the person to fill this role)

- Meeting protocols, including length of meetings, timing of breaks, and attentiveness to the person who has the floor

- Decision-making procedures: consensus, majority, or supermajority

Decision making by consensus implies that the entire group will assent. If there is not agreement by the group, the facilitator will seek modification of a proposal that meets the needs of all participants until a consensus is achieved. The process of consensus does not rely on formal rules of proce-dure, such as Robert's Rules of Order, with its attendant motions, amend-ments, and amendments to amendments. Rather, the group as a whole seeks to find a proposal that is acceptable to the entire group. The weakness of the consensus model is that a single person can impede the progress of the entire group. There are times, however valuable consensus may be, that it is neces-sary to resolve an issue and move on.

In those matters requiring a vote, a majority or a supermajority can decide the matter. A majority—particularly a slender one—can be a perilous course for any decision-making body that is addressing profound community issues. Where widespread public support is imperative, a majority of 51% of one committee is hardly the source of communitywide confidence. Moreover, the presence or absence of a single member will influence the existence of a sim-ple majority. An alternative to simple majority is the "supermajority," a re-quirement that a large majority of members, typically between 66% and 80%, agree on a disputed matter before the issue is regarded as settled.

To the maximum extent possible, consensus is helpful. But at critical points in the Task Force deliberations, some alternative to consensus may be necessary. Without such an alternative, the progress of the Task Force is sub-ject to the veto power of a single member who may be pursuing a personal agenda. On the other hand, a Task Force recommendation from a bare major-ity of members will have little credibility with the superintendent and board. A reasonable rule of thumb for consensus is 80%. It isn't unanimous, but it represents the strong conviction of the vast majority of participants.

Task Force Leadership

Task force leadership is a delicate issue. It is not unusual for a talented and well-informed person to be selected as the chair of a Task Force. Then, when a contentious issue arises on which the leader's experience, judgment, and information would be essential, the leader is expected to be impartial. This denies both the Task Force and the leader essential opportunities for contribution and collaboration. A better option for Task Force leadership may be the division of Task Force leadership into two roles: convening and facilitation. A Task Force member can convene the meetings, communicate with members, and serve as a liaison between the Task Force and the district leadership. During the meeting, however, an independent facilitator can allow all Task Force members to have equal voice and vote. Moreover, the independent facilitator can synthesize discussions and decisions so that each meeting ends with a verbal synthesis of the discussion and the next meeting begins with a written record of previous decisions. Finally, an independent facilitator who is experienced in accountability system design can help the Task Force learn from the experiences of other school systems and enable the Task Force to focus on the issues that are most important to that community.

Conclusion

Every reader who has served on a bungled committee, failed task force, or other unproductive group will undoubtedly have grave reservations about the prospect of entrusting accountability to the diverse Task Force described in this chapter. "Why not leave it to the experts? Surely the assessment and testing office can handle this job better than a bunch of laypeople!" These concerns deserve consideration, but they are ultimately unpersuasive as a rationale for abandoning the critical role that collaboration plays in the creation and maintenance of the accountability system. There is indeed a role for expertise, but that is in research, facilitation, and the suggestions for the framework of the system. There is no substitute for the ownership and creative energy of the Accountability Task Force.

CHAPTER 5

Accountability and Academic Standards
The Essential Connection

Beyond the Bell Curve

There are two fundamental choices in the manner in which students, schools, teachers, administrators, and education in general can be evaluated: standards or the bell curve. However much one may despise the standards movement or find individual academic and professional standards that are poorly constructed, it is essential that everyone who embraces a condemnation of standards fully understand the alternative. Without standards, we return to the bell curve in which performance is not judged on its merit but only on its competitive success. Without standards, the question is not "Did our students learn to read at an appropriate level?" but, rather, "Did our children have higher scores than a neighboring district or better scores than the average of districts in the nation?" Without standards, policymakers do not know if a school is successful, if leaders are effective, if teachers are responsible, or if students are learning; the policymakers only know who beat whom.

The bell curve, or more properly, the normal distribution, is a useful device in statistics and probability. It is, however, inaccurate and unsupportable as the foundation of an effective educational accountability system. Because of its dependence on rankings and the moving target called the "norm," or the average performance of students, teachers, and schools, the systems based on the bell curve provide the worst of all possible worlds. For low-performing schools, these systems shed little light on how to improve, but only report the dreadful ranking compared to other schools. For high-performing schools, the bell curve offers no real analysis of academic strengths and weaknesses but only the inappropriate complacency that accompanies the assurance that there are other schools with lower scores. This book began with the premise that the purpose of accountability is the improvement of student achievement. If that is our purpose, then the bell curve fails to assist us in the pursuit of our objective. This chapter provides the fundamental case for standards as the rational alternative to the bell curve and the application of standards in a holistic accountability system.

The Bell Curve in Student Achievement

Consider a mathematical standard in which students are expected to "find the area of a triangle." In a standards-based system, the student has not achieved the standard until he or she can successfully determine the area of a triangle. If a student is able to accomplish the task successfully along with the vast majority of other students in the class, that one student is not heaped in the middle of a distribution and labeled as the "50th percentile." Rather, the student has achieved the standard. This is the only thing that matters.

Consider the situation in which there is only one student in the class who is progressing toward the standard but still has not achieved proficiency in that standard. The other students are not progressing toward the standard. The one student who is making progress toward the standard should not be recognized as achieving the 99th percentile with all the glory and honor associated with such an exalted position. Rather, that student along with all the students in that class has not yet met the standard and every single one of them needs additional work to achieve the standard.

The norm may change from year to year as testing companies publish data with different numbers of "average" achievement by students, but the standard—to add, subtract, multiply, divide, and (in the present case) find the area of geometric shapes—does not change. It would, after all, be scant comfort to an engineering company (and to the tenants of a building that engineering company might construct) if its newest hire were unable to properly calculate the load-bearing ability of the parking lot but the engineer was proudly able to say, "But my math abilities are better than those of most of my peers!" In the real world, we are much less interested in how people fare relative to one another. What matters is only the central question: Can they do the job?

The bell curve, in sum, presumes differences in academic achievement that can be irrelevant and misleading. Although tests based on the bell curve, commonly called "norm-referenced tests," provide a neat ranking and sorting of students, the tests fail to answer the fundamental question of whether the students are proficient or whether they need additional assistance.

The Bell Curve in Accountability Policy

The same problems associated with the application of the bell curve in the classroom plague accountability policy. By ranking schools against each other, systems based on the bell curve can provide rankings and create interesting labels. My favorite category label is "Schools in Need," known in that district as the "SIN Schools." Yet however elaborate the rankings or creative the labels, these systems do not tell us if schools are successful in educating students. It is entirely possible that even a high-ranking school has many areas in need of improvement and that a low-ranking school has areas of successful practice.

Ideally, the analysis of schools, teachers, and administrators should have the same characteristics as an accurate assessment of students. Such an analysis must be fair, consistent, and accurate. The only way to meet these criteria is with a set of standards that are clear, immutable, and precise. The path to success in an effective accountability system is not "beating Central High School" or even beating the average of other schools in the state. Rather, the path to success lies in the achievement of clear objectives that do not change, that are clear for all participants in the system, and that are measured with accuracy.

Using Bell Curve Tests in a Holistic Accountability System

Does this mean that norm-referenced tests have no place in a holistic accountability system? Not necessarily. Many states and school districts require the use of nationally normed tests as part of their accountability systems, and it is possible to use these tests in a holistic accountability system with the following provisions. First, the focus must be on proficiency, not ranking. In other words, "percentage correct" is far more meaningful than "percentile rank" as an indicator of what students know and are able to do. Just as teachers can determine what satisfactory performance is on their tests without resorting to meaningless comparisons, so too can school leaders and policymakers determine what scores in the accountability system represent proficiency. Performance, not ranking, is what matters. Second, the test must be accepted for what it is: a single measurement of student achievement, not the definitive measurement of student achievement. Thoughtful critics have amply described the flaws in standardized tests (Neill, 1998; Popham, 2000). But the fundamental flaw in standardized tests is not merely in their construction but in their inappropriate use. Even the best test designed by thoughtful people with great care and professionalism suffers from the inherent limitation that it is a single measurement and thus cannot be used to make an inference about a human being. No responsible medical professional would draw a definitive conclusion from a single measurement of blood pressure but would, instead, take that measurement several times and augment that information with other tests and measurements before coming to a conclusion. Such a practice does not disparage the inventor of the blood pressure cuff; similarly, the inherent limitations of any single standardized test are not intended to cast aspersions on the integrity or professionalism of test designers. Their thoughtfully designed tests can be used in holistic accountability systems, but they must be used as one measurement among many and cannot be used as the definitive and sole indicator of student success.

Standards for Student Achievement

The most important characteristic of standards-based assessments is their fundamental purpose: the improvement of student achievement. This stands in marked contrast to the typical purposes of standardized tests. Students, parents, and policymakers have been conditioned for generations to view tests as evaluative in nature. The tests answer questions such as "How am I doing?" or "Did we beat the neighboring school?" or "Are these students better than the national average?" The fundamental question, however, should be "How can students and schools improve their achievement?" The last question is only addressed when the assessment is designed to provide feedback that is, in Grant Wiggins's (1988) phrase, "educative."

In effectively crafted standards-based performance assessments, the criteria for evaluation are elaborated in a rubric, or scoring guide. These criteria, best expressed in student-accessible language, give students feedback not only on the extent to which their performance was proficient but also on how to improve. The best rubrics amplify the descriptions of nonproficient scores with specific guidance for improvement. Students at the secondary level have a common answer for the parents' question, "Why did you get that grade?" In the 49 states and four continents where I have posed that question to students, the most common answer is "I don't know." Assessments that are designed to be educative, by contrast, require a different answer. Students have a scoring guide that does not merely render a judgment but which includes words such as these extracted from a secondary school science rubric:

> Your Score: 2—Progressing, but not yet proficient. The data were accurately plotted on the graph, the graph labels were accurate, and all laboratory safety procedures were correctly followed. The lab report was incomplete and did not meet science-writing standards. In order to be proficient, section four of the lab report must accurately report the data from the graph and explain the relationships of the variables (temperature and melting point) that were observed. Section five of the lab report must be free of errors in grammar and punctuation. The project will receive a score of "Proficient" if it is corrected and resubmitted within three days.

In sum, the standards-based assessments are strikingly different from traditional tests. Success is a function of meeting a standard, not defeating a colleague. Success requires demonstration, not guesswork. Success is achieved through learning, not gamesmanship. Success is achieved with feedback and multiple opportunities, not mastery attained before the class began. Indeed, the function of standards-based assessments is the promotion of student success, not merely the identification of success and failure.

Standards for Curriculum

Standards implementation inevitably leads to curriculum reform, including the provision of intensive assistance for small groups of students who are not initially meeting standards. Another essential element of curriculum reform is the systematic use of standards in the description of courses. At the very least, this means that every class (particularly in a middle school, junior high, or high school) is listed in a course catalogue and is associated with one or more standards established by the district. Some districts, for example, have standards in statistics but no classes in it. On the other hand, they have classes in psychology, sociology, and photography, but no standards are associated with those classes.

If standards are to become more than a slogan, then one of two things must happen. Either the classes that are not associated with standards are no longer taught or—a better alternative—the teachers of those classes creatively identify ways their classes can help students achieve academic standards. For example, statistics standards can clearly be met in a number of sociology, ethnic studies, psychology, and social studies classes. The same is true of many language arts and civics standards. The photography class could be linked to standards in mathematics, language arts, and civics. The bottom line remains, however, that classes not linked to standards do not make a contribution to the goals of the district and should not be taught.

Standards implementation requires a compartmentalized curriculum. By compartmentalization I mean the reduction of some academic subjects into smaller blocks. There should be no such thing as "9th-grade mathematics" or "10th-grade English." Rather, standards that these classes have traditionally comprised should be taught in units ranging in time from a few weeks to a full semester. It might be possible that some students would take two classes to complete all those requirements—the time traditionally used for a full class. Other students, however, may need four, five, or even six units to achieve the same level of standards.

This is most evident in mathematics classes. The notion that every 9th and 10th grader should take the same algebra class is simply preposterous. A number of students enter high school without knowing multiplication tables and

1. A teacher can describe the teacher's philosophy of education and demonstrate its relationship to the teacher's practice.

2. A teacher understands how students learn and develop and applies that knowledge in the teacher's practice.

3. A teacher teaches students with respect for their individual and cultural characteristics.

4. A teacher knows the teacher's content area and how to teach it.

5. A teacher facilitates, monitors, and assesses student learning.

6. A teacher creates and maintains a learning environment in which all students are actively engaged and contributing members.

7. A teacher works as a partner with parents, families, and the community.

8. A teacher participates in and contributes to the teaching profession.

Figure 5.1. Standards for Alaska's Teachers

have little preparation for algebra class. The traditional system requires that these students take a class for which they are hopelessly ill prepared and then brands those students as failures in mathematics. A better approach is to permit these students to achieve high school mathematics standards through a number of different classes, including not only traditional academic classes but also application classes, vocational classes, and interdisciplinary classes. Those students still have to achieve the algebra standard but they do so by taking a variety of classes—not by taking a "dumbed-down" curriculum.

The goal of a standards-based curriculum is not to tell students how to achieve standards but, rather, to provide a broad menu of alternatives that meet the needs of students who require additional instruction as well as those who have already achieved the standards and appreciate further enrichment. The practical effect of this system is that students who need to spend more time to accomplish the graduation standards will take fewer electives. Does this mean that a student who needs extra math and English classes in order to achieve high school graduation might not have time in his or her curriculum for band and drama? That is precisely what it means.

Standards for Teaching Practice

Every state has embraced some version of academic content standards, with 49 states establishing these expectations of what students should know at the

1. An administrator provides leadership for an educational organization.

2. An administrator guides instruction and supports an effective learning environment.

3. An administrator oversees the implementation of curriculum.

4. An administrator coordinates services that support student growth and development.

5. An administrator provides for staffing and professional development to meet student learning needs.

6. An administrator uses assessment and evaluation information about students, staff, and the community in making decisions.

7. An administrator communicates with diverse groups and individuals with clarity and sensitivity.

8. An administrator acts in accordance with established laws, policies, procedures, and good business practices.

9. An administrator understands the influence of social, cultural, political, and economic forces on the educational environment and uses this knowledge to serve the needs of children, families, and communities.

10. An administrator facilitates the participation of parents and families as partners in the education of children.

Figure 5.2. State of Alaska Standards for Administrators

state level and one (Iowa) requiring school districts to establish standards. Only a few states (Alaska is a notable example) have been as diligent in establishing standards for the adults in the system as they have in the establishment of standards for students. If standards and accountability are to reach their potential of mutual reinforcement and synergy, then the standards-setting effort cannot conclude with academic expectations for the children in the system. Standards for teachers, leaders, policymakers, and (dare I say it?) parents and communities are all integral elements of student success. Just as an effective accountability system includes measurement of academic success (systemwide indicators) and the strategies that lead to that success (school-based indicators), so do effective standards include both the expectations of students and the requirements for teaching and leadership that help students reach those expectations.

Examples of standards for teachers and administrators are presented in Figures 5.1 and 5.2, respectively. These examples are taken from standards established by the Alaska Department of Education (1997a, 1997b).

Standards for Policymakers and Leaders

The role of the board of education is to set policy. Such a statement may seem so pedestrian that it is superfluous. Nevertheless, the number of times in which a board of education engages in the day-to-day administration of schools makes it clear that the difference between policy and administration is neither obvious nor overstated. This difference lies at the heart of effective board membership and progressive policy leadership. Boards that become immersed in administration cannot lead policy.

One of the most frequent frustrations that I hear from superintendents and other senior leaders of schools throughout the nation is the failure of school boards to confine their work to committed policy development. "I've got four out of seven board members who are former teachers and administrators," one superintendent lamented, "and all of them believe that their service on the school board is their chance to finally become the superintendent."

Board members see things differently. "I want to be supportive and stick to policy issues," a frustrated board member reports, "but the superintendent treats us like children. Every time we ask a legitimate question, the superintendent huffs and insists that we really don't need to know such things. It's infuriating." Board members have a legitimate need to create policy based on accurate and contemporary information. Superintendents have an equally legitimate responsibility to exercise administrative leadership in the implementation of policy. Both roles involve leadership; both roles require accurate information. Neither role can operate in isolation. The issue is not "Who is really in charge?" but, rather, "What are our roles?" Both the board and superintendent exercise leadership, but policy leadership must be clearly distinguished from administrative leadership.

How can these two roles be reconciled? A comprehensive accountability system can provide board members with a blend of very specific school-level information, along with qualitative and narrative data that puts this information in proper context. The same accountability system can also give superintendents, senior leaders, and other members of a school community important information on which they can base initiatives that improve student achievement. There exist some methods that school board members can use to help districts design and implement a comprehensive accountability system. These methods include building the system architecture with clear accountability indicators and deciding when and how often data should be reported and how it should be used. The school board also plays a critical role in using accountability as a permanent framework for all other district programs and keeping the focus by prioritizing issues within the framework of the accountability system.

Standards for Accountability Systems

Any accountability system must itself be accountable. This means that the validity and reliability of accountability measures cannot be assumed but must constantly be measured and subjected to challenge, improvement, and revision. This emphatically does not mean that every student must take identical tests in order for the achievement of standards to be demonstrated. Instead, districts should consider the concept of concurrent validity tests, in which teacher-created assessments are the primary determinant of standards achievement and districtwide assessments are performed to obtain random samples of students. Samples of students can take a districtwide assessment (also based on the same standards), and the results of these assessments can be compared to the data from the standards achievement reports. Although some disparities may occur due to differences in the forms of the assessments, the results should be consistent in a very high percentage of cases. If a teacher is reporting that 95% of his or her students are meeting standards but a districtwide assessment performed with a sample of students from that class indicated that only 50% of students are meeting standards, then such a disparity should be investigated. However, my experience is that classroom teachers tend to be more rigorous in determining whether or not students meet standards. Teacher-created classroom-level assessments are more likely to indicate a student does not meet the academic content standards than are the results of a standardized test. Traditional assessments might label that student as "average" and hence give that student the false sense of security that he or she is "satisfactory," whereas the standards-based performance assessment will clearly label the student's performance as "progressing" or "not meeting standards," even if a comparison to other students might indicate that the student's work is above average.

The use of this concurrent validity system saves enormous resources for the district. In most cases, public confidence will increase when the districtwide test results show a higher level of achievement than had been reported by the teachers.

Conclusion

When describing educational standards to parents and committee members, I frequently refer to standards as "the rules of the game." At first, some people are taken aback at the nonchalant reference to a game as an inappropriately flippant metaphor in a serious discussion of education. That is precisely the point. In the inconsequential games of the playground, we take great care to specify rules with clear expectations and consistent guidelines. We owe no less to the serious matters of educational accountability. Supreme Court Justice Powell famously described pornography as something that he could not define but "I know it when I see it." Such a pornography definition characterizes too many accountability systems that lack clear standards. Such systems cannot really describe educational achievement but are nevertheless able to generate ponderous reports about the subject after the data have been examined. If the goal of accountability is the improvement of achievement, then the accountability system must apply standards—clear expectations of what students, teachers, and leaders are expected to do—before the system is implemented. Every child (and every teacher who has spent time on playground duty) knows that a game without rules is a certain invitation to fights and tears. Accountability without standards has the same inevitable result.

CHAPTER **6**

Models of Effective Accountability Systems

Holistic accountability is not a new idea. Some progressive school systems have already created the models that are improving student achievement and yielding excellent information for school leaders and policymakers. This chapter catalogues a few of these exemplary systems.

Components of an Effective Accountability Model

All of the model accountability systems described in this chapter share some common characteristics. These include systemwide principles and values and the use of a common architecture of the accountability system. One striking characteristic of the best accountability systems is that they emphasize principles over indicators. That is, these systems may diverge sharply on the nature of the tests or other indicators that were chosen to represent effective academic achievement, but they are quite similar with respect to the principles and values that govern their selection.

This is a reasonable question to consider: Why should principles and values play a role in what is, in theory, a statistical, objective, psychometric pursuit? The answer is that the stakeholders in an accountability system may disagree violently on the selection of tests, standards, or academic indicators, but they tend to agree on principles and values. For example, most stakeholders tend to agree on the following principles: accuracy, fairness, relevance, specificity, respect for diversity, and clarity. (Please see Step 2 in Chapter 7 for a description of each principle.)

My colleagues at the International Center for Educational Accountability have worked with school systems that developed scores of principles and values, but all school systems tend to find common ground in such areas as fairness and accuracy. Although this may appear obvious to the casual observer, it is not obvious in the context of a contentious discussion of educational accountability. Only when principles and values are established first is it clear that our disagreements over specific tests and our grievances over past history pale in comparison to our consensus with respect to the principles of fairness and accuracy.

Accountability System Design

Closely related to the principles of the holistic accountability system is the design of the system. Form follows function. Thus the design of an effective accountability system consists of three distinct parts: systemwide indicators, school-based indicators, and qualitative indicators. Most accountability systems contain only the first of these three essential elements. Test scores, attendance, and other systemwide variables are the sum and substance of most accountability systems.

Case Studies in Effective Accountability Practice

The three case studies in this chapter represent vastly different school systems with remarkably different needs. Nevertheless, each of these systems demonstrates a strong commitment to the principles of holistic accountability. Despite their differences, each Task Force developed remarkably similar principles that guided their deliberations, and thus each system employs similar accountability system designs. Our case studies are of a large urban system and two suburban systems. Although none of them uses the word "holistic" to describe their accountability systems, all have successfully applied the principles described in this book and thus are instructive models for leaders of state and local school systems of any size.

Wayne Township, Indiana

Wayne Township is near Indianapolis, Indiana. Despite its name implying a quaint suburb, the school system is beset with the same urban problems that affect many larger school districts. With the largest three-year high school in the state of Indiana and a number of model programs, the district superintendent, Dr. Terry Thompson, was continually in search of methods to improve student achievement. The statewide test results were showing signs of trouble, and a new high school graduation examination was on the horizon. Without a focused effort, many of Wayne Township's students would gather credits in school but face a future without a high school diploma. As with many districts, there had been a strong tradition of site-based decision making. One of the first jobs confronting the Accountability Task Force was to clarify what decisions would continue to be site based and what decisions would be reserved for the central administration. The accountability structure of systemwide goals and school-based goals quickly resolved this dilemma. The board of education had established four goals that had been affirmed year after year. These formed the foundation for the systemwide goals. Each school building, however, was free to select its school-based goals depending on an analysis of its own needs. In some schools, parent and community involvement were significant challenges, whereas in others, active parents had had the program on "automatic pilot" for years. In schools, high mobility rates made it important to consider the short-term performance of students who might only be enrolled for a few weeks, whereas in other schools, fall-to-spring comparisons or even year-to-year comparisons of student performance were possible. The freedom to select goals at the school level came with a price: exposure. For the first time, every school principal, and indeed the general public, was able to view a single document that revealed the goals of all the other schools. Rather than view the list of test scores typically published in the newspaper, each school now had a much fuller context. They knew what each school had done to achieve (or to fail to achieve) its goals. This detailed elaboration of the strategies schools employed encouraged cooperation between building administrators and site teams. The most successful goals and practices were emulated, and as principals viewed the goals of each building, the next generation of building-based goals became more specific, clear, and meaningful. Perhaps the best result of the Wayne Township accountability system has been the focus on data at the building level. In every single building, monthly and quarterly progress on school goals is apparent in charts that adorn the walls of the hallways and cafeterias. Students and teachers in Wayne Township know that accountability is not merely a list of test scores but is a living system designed to improve achievement. Because the charts are not sequestered in the principal's office but displayed in areas frequented by students, the clear messages to every child are "We are not last year's test scores" and "We are getting better every day."

Milwaukee, Wisconsin

The second case study is Milwaukee Public Schools, the 16th-largest school system in the nation. As with many urban systems, Milwaukee has a high number of students in poverty, and its schools are often presumed to be places of urban blight. Although Milwaukee does suffer from many urban problems, it is also the site of the some of the most remarkably successful urban schools in the nation. The accountability system in Milwaukee was initiated under the leadership of Superintendent Robert Jasna. Although three additional superintendents have taken the reins of the school district since Mr. Jasna's retirement and the majority of the board of education has changed significantly, the accountability system has remained intact. Perhaps the reason for the endurance of the system is that it was designed by a Task Force that represented many different stakeholders and, when presented to a school board that was known for its frequent divisiveness, the accountability system was passed unanimously. The design of the system in Milwaukee is common to all the case studies: Systemwide indicators represented the goals that the school board wanted every school to accomplish; school-based indicators represented the individual strategies of each school; the school narrative included a page of comments that helped readers of the accountability report better understand the quantitative data.

During the initial development of the Milwaukee accountability system, some board members expressed concern over the freedom with which individual schools could select their building-based goals. "Why, they could just choose anything and give themselves easy goals," one board member cautioned. The compromise reached allowed the schools unlimited choice of school-based goals during the first year of the program, and then choice within a board-approved menu of goals after the first year. Because the menu of more than 90 school goals was based on the most effective school goals of the first year, the menu represented both the choice desired by building principals and the limits demanded by the board.

The reports of the Milwaukee accountability system provided notable insights for educational leaders in that city and throughout the nation. First, the city was the first to identify its "90/90/90" schools, those buildings where 90% or more of the students were eligible for free or reduced lunch, 90% of the students were members of ethnic minorities, and 90% of the students met or exceeded the district reading standard. By identifying the common characteristics of these schools, it was possible for the district to replicate its best practices in many other schools (Milwaukee Public Schools, 1999; Reeves, 2000a). Second, the Milwaukee system provided extraordinary specificity and clarity for goals. Because the goals of every building were open to public discussion and review, general goals such as "improve parental involvement" or "improve student achievement" were rendered far more specific with each succeeding year of the accountability system. Rather than sliding by with the easy goals feared by some board members, the schools aggressively chose such challenging and specific goals as "Increase the percentage of parents who volunteer 20 or more hours of school service" and "Increase the percentage of students who meet or exceed the state math proficiency requirement." Third, and most important, the accountability system forced district administrators to come to grips with a problem that plagues school systems large and small: different ways of recording and reporting the same data. Because everything from attendance to dropout rates to mobility to advanced placement class enrollment had been inconsistent, the reports of those data from schools had little value. With the advent of the accountability system, precise definitions were applied to every measurement and, for the first time, virtually every administrator was applying the same rules to record and report school data. Did the accountability system transform Milwaukee into an educational wonderland? Certainly not. But the accountability system did provide the leaders, board members, and general public the most detailed and systematic understanding of student achievement that they had ever had. One of the members of the Accountability Task Force spoke volumes when he admitted, "I just didn't know that it was this complicated." One person at a time, community members, reporters, and other observers became aware that in Milwaukee, accountability meant far more than a litany of test scores.

Riverview Gardens, Missouri

The third case study, Riverview Gardens, Missouri, is located outside St. Louis. As with Wayne Township, the district has many significant urban challenges. The structure of the Riverview Gardens accountability system was quite similar to the other systems described in this chapter. There were systemwide goals supported by clearly articulated and widely shared school-based goals. One distinguishing characteristic of the Riverview Gardens system, however, was its emphasis on frequent feedback to teachers and administrators during the year. The superintendent, Dr. Chris Wright, initiated a program called "Write Focus" in which students in every single class were required to complete a formal writing assessment every month in every class. Part of the rationale for this program was the observation made from other accountability systems, such as in Milwaukee, that increases in student writing assessments were associated with improvements in student achievement. At the end of the first year of the program, the district received wide recognition for dramatic increases in its test scores, with particularly sharp gains in social studies and science. Outside observers might have attributed the gains to "test prep" or other questionable schemes, but the Riverview Gardens records made clear that the thinking, reasoning, analysis, and communications skills that students had built through their writing assessments in a multitude of different classes had paid significant dividends. *St. Louis Post-Dispatch* published a lead editorial titled "Answers in Riverview Gardens" (2000) and encouraged schools throughout the area to follow the lead that Dr. Wright and her colleagues had established. Significantly, the district did not rest on its laurels but used data from the accountability system to identify those schools that had the highest degrees of implementation of the writing program and to note that their performance was superior to schools with lower degrees of implementation. This enabled the district to deploy scarce central office resources strategically to provide help where it was most needed. Moreover, it sent the message to everyone concerned that accountability was not a device to label and rank schools but was a system devoted to the improvement of student achievement. Finally, it is noteworthy that the same superintendent who created a new accountability system and was recognized as a leader in improving student achievement also received national recognition for good labor relationships. The notion that effective accountability relies on punitive measures, authoritarian rule, or mindless test prep is belied by the success of Riverview Gardens.

Conclusion

There is a paradox in the design of holistic accountability systems. Although the purpose of accountability is the improvement of educational achievement, no accountability system by itself can possibly accomplish that objective. The best that can happen is that the accountability system provides information in the never-ending search for the antecedents of excellence, those professional practices and leadership policies that are consistently associated with improved student learning. Some of the findings of these three districts were strikingly similar: Poor children can excel academically, and frequent writing assessment is one of the best professional practices to improve thinking, reasoning, analysis, and, yes, even test scores. The political environments of these cases were strikingly different, with strong board cohesion in Wayne Township and deep board divisions in Milwaukee. The composition of the Task Forces were different, with prominent ministers and a board member participating in the Wayne Township Task Force, strong union representation on the Milwaukee Task Force, and an adaptation of a previously existing school improvement team structure in Riverview Gardens. The Milwaukee and Riverview Gardens plans required half a dozen Task Force meetings for completion, whereas the Wayne Township plan was completed in half that time. But all three plans have common elements that are far more important than their differences. First, and most important, all three accountability systems place test scores in the broader context of a variety of systemwide and building-based accountability indicators. Second, all three systems provide varying degrees of school-based choice in the selection of accountability goals. Third, all three are living systems, with continuous improvements in the quality, rigor, and relevance of their instructional strategies. Conversations about accountability are opportunities for professionals to learn how to improve their practice rather than defensive encounters marked by rhetorical thrusts and parries. No one familiar with these three systems would call them perfect, but anyone familiar with educational accountability would acknowledge that they are exemplary models of collaboration and effectiveness in an extraordinarily challenging field.

CHAPTER 7

Ten Steps to Creating a Holistic Accountability System

Although every holistic accountability system will have unique character-istics that reflect the individual needs of the schools and community, there are consistent procedures for the establishment of the accountability system that will improve collaboration and save time. This chapter describes these steps and provides a rationale each of them. It is a good idea for the Accountability Task Force to review this chapter before deliberations begin so that each member of the Task Force has a clear idea of the context of their work.

Step 1. Collaboration: Establish the Accountability Task Force

Developing a holistic accountability system is a labor-intensive process. The first step in undertaking this work is the establishment of an Accountability Task Force. The Task Force will have primary responsibility for coordination and oversight as the accountability system is developed and implemented. Because Task Force members will have a number of difficult, time-consuming responsibilities, it is important to make this clear to potential Task Force participants before they agree to join. Members should be willing to attend a minimum of six 2-hour meetings during the design phase of their work, and then participate in quarterly meetings thereafter. Terms of service are typically two years.

The Task Force reports to the superintendent who, in turn, reports to the board of education. The political dynamics of some school systems are such that the Accountability Task Force reports directly to the board of education. In chartering the Accountability Task Force, the board must make these reporting relationships clear.

Leaders want to collaborate; they also know that they will be held responsible for the implementation of vision and achievement of the mission of their school system. Although they want to honor the need for collaboration among many stakeholders, leaders and policymakers frequently find excuses to make the development of the accountability system a private endeavor. I have worked in some school systems in which the superintendent says, "Look, I've attended a seminar on accountability systems. Why can't I just write the system and submit it to the board?" The answer to this question lies not in any particular affection I have for committees and task forces but, rather, with the essential issue of ownership. Who owns the accountability system, anyway? If accountability is the exclusive creation of the superintendent and board, then other stakeholders, such as teachers, administrators, parents, students, and the community, can be expected to show little enthusiasm for it. "Here they go again," the excluded stakeholders will sigh, as they watch one more initiative come and go. The reasons for excluding stakeholders from the accountability process are rarely pernicious. Well-intentioned, thoughtful, and (usually) collaborative school leaders have explained their reluctance to engage a broadly based Accountability Task Force with explanations such as the following:

- "This is really about testing and assessment, and that's too technical a field for most laypeople."

- "We can't allow parents and business representatives on the Accountability Task Force to act as if they are supervising principals and teachers."

- "We have site-based decision making, and a community Task Force that designs an accountability system will take away the authority of the site councils."

- "The goals of the district should be set by the board and superintendent, not by the stakeholders."

- "If we bring all the stakeholders together, they will never be able to agree to anything."

- "If I let the teacher's union sit at the table, then administrators won't join in; and if I allow principals, then the union won't participate. It's best just to have the central office and board make these decisions."

- "Our board already knows what they want. Why would they listen to a group of stakeholders?"

The resistance to stakeholder involvement is not unlike the subtle resistance to parental involvement in the classroom. "I know that they mean well," the reasoning goes, "but shouldn't we leave the education of our children up to the experts?" The answer, at least in a democracy, is a resounding no. Our history and form of government place extraordinary trust in the common sense of the people. The overwhelming majority of school board members and legislators are citizen volunteers. They exercise enormous power with regard to the resources and policies of school systems, and therefore school leaders exclude citizen leaders from accountability deliberations at some peril. What a school administrator might see as a reasonable division of labor ("Leave the details to the experts!") can strike a board member or legislator as contemptuous arrogance. The victims of such misunderstandings are children and schools who are denied the resources they need to be successful.

If, on the other hand, a broadly representative Task Force is both the author of the accountability system and the group that presents accountability information to the board and public, then a different organizational dynamic is present. It is no longer the typical meeting in which the administration presents (and, more often than not, defends) its information in a two-way exchange with the board. Rather, the Accountability Task Force, including teachers, administrators, parents, and other stakeholders, presents information to the school leadership. The board and superintendent are, literally and figuratively, on the same side of the table.

Step 2. Lead With Values: Create Accountability Principles

What are the essential principles of an effective accountability system? The definitive answer rests with the Accountability Task Force for each school system. It is imperative, however, that the Task Force reaches a consensus on values before proceeding to the other steps in this chapter. Only by making reference to agreed-on values and principles can the inevitable controversies over structure and details be resolved. For example, if there is agreement on "accuracy" as a principle, then the accountability system must ensure that the results that are reported on student test scores are not merely the average as reported by the test companies but that the test scores accurately reflect the performance of the students who were actually in the schools. If there is agreement on "clarity" as a principle, then the accountability reports must be in a format that does not require a degree in statistics to understand. If there is agreement on "accessibility," then the accountability data cannot be secret or difficult to obtain.

Although every Task Force will create its own terminology and definitions of principles, the following seven principles reflect the input of many diverse board members, community members, teachers, students, and school leaders. This list is by no means exhaustive, but should serve to stimulate discussion by the Task Force as it creates its own Task Forces. These principles include

(a) congruence, (b) respect for diversity, (c) accuracy, (d) specificity, (e) feedback for continuous improvement, (f) universality, and (g) fairness.

Congruence

First, an effective accountability system must be congruent. That is, the accountability system must be compatible with the rewards and incentives already in place in the school district. The most frequent incongruity in accountability systems is the disparity between personnel evaluation systems (often rather arbitrary and based on administrative efficiency and discipline practices) and educational accountability (often based on test scores). An effective accountability system must provide the same incentives for educational excellence that personnel evaluation systems embody.

If the principle of congruence is to be implemented effectively, then accountability must be a framework within which all other plans, programs, and documents fit. The accountability plan establishes what is important enough to measure and report. It focuses on excellence and equity. Matters that do not fall within this purview are probably not worth the attention of policymakers and school leaders. Properly implemented, a comprehensive accountability plan can become a source of vital information for all other plans and initiatives in the district. Moreover, it can be a filter through which prospective new programs and ideas must pass. If new initiatives do not support the accountability system, then school officials should seriously question whether or not they should be taken on.

Respect for Diversity

The second principle of effective accountability systems is respect for the diversity of individual schools. "Diversity" must be more than the slogan of the decade. It must be a practical consideration in the reality of complex school systems. Diversity includes not only the apparent differences between students but also the differences that exist among schools, curricula, programs, cultures, learning styles, and a host of other important sources of diversity. A school system might include magnet and specialty schools such as language immersion schools, schools for the arts, schools of technology, and International Baccalaureate programs, as well as schools designed to improve the performance of academically disadvantaged students.

As important as diversity is in principle, there is great danger for student learning when the term becomes politicized and thus is little more than a code word for lower expectations among disadvantaged students. Diversity can and must certainly apply to strategies, but there cannot be diversity with regard to the standards of performance expected of students.

Accuracy

Third, the accountability system must be accurate. This means more than the typical "reliability and validity" required for educational tests. After all, there are many tests that appear to be valid and reliable but do not measure adequately the attributes an accountability system seeks to evaluate. The principle of accuracy requires not only that the measurements themselves are correct but also that the measurements are used appropriately.

Test scores fail to reflect the educational efforts that are the "antecedents of excellence": professional development of the staff, involvement by the parents, engagement of the students, excellence in assessment and instructional practices, and a climate of safety and educational achievement in the schools. An effective system must measure all these indicators if it is to give policymakers the information they need to distinguish between effective and ineffective programs, policies, and practices.

Specificity

Fourth, an accountability system must be specific. The people responsible for the education of our children must have a clear idea of what they must do to help all students achieve. Any ambiguity leaves the demoralized staff and school leadership guessing what they should do and frequently working exceedingly hard at precisely the wrong things.

The practical implication of the principle of specificity is that the accountability system must focus on practices of leaders and teachers, not merely on test scores. Teachers will embrace accountability only if the system gives them the ability to improve student learning. If the system merely blames them for the effects of the educational system, then resistance, rather than cooperation, will result.

Feedback for Continuous Improvement

The fifth principle of effective accountability is feedback for continuous improvement. This means that accountability system data are both summative and formative. Accountability data summarize the results of school improvement and student achievement but also use the results to inform school improvement decisions and initiatives.

This continuous use of feedback is what Dr. Jeff Howard, president of the Efficacy Institute, calls the "Nintendo Effect." He notes that many children who have been labeled as having Attention Deficit Disorder and are assumed to be unable to concentrate will play Nintendo games for hours at a time. Why? Because they receive immediate and relevant feedback. "How many students," Dr. Howard asks, "would play Nintendo if they didn't receive the score for several months?" Indeed, how many adults would find a process meaningful if the feedback never came to them in either a meaningful or timely fashion? In the context of educational accountability, students, teachers, and leaders need feedback that meets the same criteria.

Universality

Universality is the sixth accountability element. It is unusual indeed to find a school system in which there are as many standards for adults as there are for children and as many accountability indicators for the central office, board, and parents as there are for teachers. Comprehensive accountability systems do not deserve to use the words "comprehensive" or "accountability" if only the performance of children is measured. Teaching and leadership practices, as well as the influences of board policymakers and, to be sure, parents, are critical elements of the system.

The principle of universality means that accountability is not simply about threatening 8-year-olds with retention unless they achieve a certain test score; it is not about threatening teachers if their students are ill prepared for a test; it is not about closing down schools and firing administrators. Accountability, when governed by the principle of universality, applies to all stakeholders—students as well as board members; parents as well as policymakers; teachers as well as administrators. The health of the patient depends not on the singular efforts of the physician, patient, supportive family, or hospital trustee; rather, all these medical stakeholders can help or hinder the successful recovery of the patient. Anything less than a universal effort undermines the health of the system. So it is with educational accountability.

Fairness

The seventh and final element of effective accountability systems is fairness. Children will not long engage in a game where the rules change and are widely regarded as unfair. If their efforts are not reflected in the score of the game, or if they are penalized for events over which they have no control, they wonder whether the game is worth the effort and sometimes quit amid tears and anger. Listen to the conversations of principals and teachers as they discuss contemporary accountability systems. These conversations will include tales about the frustrations of administering tests to students who cannot read the questions, as well as about the anger and tears of children who are entering their fifth school this year but have yet to be academically engaged. Educator discussions will also include immense pride in the unnoticed accomplishments of students and exceptional work of teachers, and perhaps a bit of cynicism about the public acknowledgment of a teacher or administrator who appears to have a greater gift for self-promotion than education.

Every teacher and parent knows that children have an innate sense of fairness. Fairness means that we understand the rules of the game, that the rules of the game are applied consistently, and that everyone has the opportunity to play by the same rules. Unlike adults, who frequently associate games with winning and losing, children know that fairness operates as a universal principle irrespective of notions of victory and defeat. Fairness and accountability is not about "beating" someone else, but it is certainly about winning the battle against inequity, injustice, and ignorance. Those victories are beyond our grasp if our students, teachers, and school leaders do not believe that they are governed fairly.

Step 3. Define the Real World: Identify the Current Accountability System

It is a delusion for any school system to believe that the Task Force will "create" an accountability system. The plain fact is that every school system already has an accountability system, even if it is not apparent. Existing accountability systems may not bear that label, but every superintendent, board member, principal, and teacher has some level of accountability right now. The problem is that these accountability methods, although implied, are often undefined, unclear, and internally inconsistent. To find their "hidden" accountability systems, members of a Task Force subcommittee should inventory the personnel evaluation forms of the district, reward and incentive systems, and current methods for imposing sanctions on schools.

If a local business group or educational foundation provides cash awards and extraordinary recognition for one sort of activity—say, dramatic performances—then we should not be very surprised if people are drawn to such activities. If a high school administrator receives greater recognition for processing paperwork accurately than for helping a student who is in an academic crisis, then it should not surprise us if the administrator responds to that reward system. If the superintendent and central office administrators can only maintain their jobs by responding to daily demands from board members for information, research, and investigations, then we should not be surprised if academic initiatives take a back seat to job security.

In an astonishing number of cases, there are clear contradictions between what school districts purport to reward and what actually garners favor or sanction. A comprehensive accountability system—if it is clearly supported by senior leaders and policymakers—can help school systems move away from espousing one set of expectations while actually rewarding quite another. An effective accountability system can help schools channel their efforts toward clear objectives and realign their reward systems to promote the results they seek. If schools want accountability systems with this kind of congruence, then Task Force members must explore both the explicit and implicit factors embedded in the district's "hidden" accountability structure.

Step 4. Design the Framework: Accountability System Architecture

Chapter 6 suggests a framework that includes three levels: systemwide indicators, school-based indicators, and a school narrative. This format, however, may not be appropriate for every system. For example, some accountability systems must be designed for a county, state, or other multidistrict system. In other cases, there is a single school for the entire system. In still other cases, the schools are so large that the accountability system must be linked to classes, departments, or other subdivisions.

Whatever the structure of your system, the accountability system architecture should be consistent with the principles of the Task Force. In addition, the structure should maintain a balance between "effect" variables such as test scores and "cause" variables such as instructional practices and leadership decisions. Finally, the accountability system architecture should balance quantitative indicators, such as numbers and percentages, and qualitative indicators, such as narrative descriptions.

Step 5. The Devil in the Details: Conduct a Critical Review of Accountability Plan Design

Working with a number of accountability groups around the nation, I have witnessed the spectacle of an elegantly designed system falling apart under the strain of some avoidable pitfalls. Although it may not be possible to foresee every potential problem, the following difficulties are those most likely to undermine the efforts of even the most diligent Task Force. Therefore, it is wise to consider these potential challenges before the ink dries on the system and it is formally proposed to the superintendent and board. Moreover, a consideration of these problems will enable the Task Force members to anticipate challenges that may come from other stakeholders and decision makers in the community.

Statistical Quicksand—Complexity Without Clarity

Decision makers want clarity, and we respond with complexity. The board wants test scores, and we insist on placing information in context and giving it meaning. They want numbers, and we provide narrative. They insist on summaries, and we find detail imperative. Because one of the unspoken laws of school administration is "One rarely wins arguments with board members," what is the school leader who wishes to support comprehensive accountability supposed to do when the board demands "accountability lite"?

Effective accountability systems focus on a few indicators, typically five or six systemwide indicators and another five or six school-based indicators. Board members get to the bottom line they seek because they can focus on the key indicators that are of most importance. Only with this degree of focus can policymakers and leaders avoid descending into the quicksand of meaningless data distinguished by their quantity and complexity more than by relevance and meaning.

The Testing Trap

Closely related to statistical quicksand is the pitfall that involves excessive focus on test results. Test results are, to be sure, an important indicator of student achievement. Test data are necessary but insufficient sources of information for analyzing educational accountability. By far the most common error in accountability systems in education today is the exclusive focus on test data without an accompanying focus on the causes of student performance (Bracey, 1999; Popham, 2000; Reeves, 2000b; "Weak Tests," 1998). The impact of the testing trap goes well beyond errors in board policy, as the board chases every program, promise, and silver bullet in order to increase last year's test scores. The classroom impact is even more insidious, as teachers frantically attempt to follow the board's demands for improved test scores and drill children on the test questions from the previous year. Even when board members have access to fair and accurate test data for one year, it is too easy to leap to the conclusion that those test results are the consequence of the current year's curriculum and instruction. Of course, learning is cumulative, and test scores are the result of several years of curriculum, instruction, and assessment strategies.

Selective Truth

The most consistent pitfall in accountability systems is the selective use of data. Although bias may be inherent in human nature, it need not be a fixture of accountability systems. The most disturbing elements of bias are the use of inflammatory, exaggerated, and inaccurate descriptions that accompany test data. I have witnessed instances of significant growth in student achievement being either ignored or suppressed, apparently because evidence of quality in public education did not conform to the election-year convictions of those whose political success depended on evidence of public education failure. Few political challengers, after all, can succeed in unseating the incumbent on the slogan "Student achievement is improving!" The need for change (such as a new occupant of a seat in the legislature or on the school board) implies a rationale for change (such as "The status quo is an abject failure"). Data to the contrary are most inconvenient for purveyors of doom.

A Distinction Without a Difference

Even the best accountability systems flounder on the issue of categories and ranking. We want to know not merely whether or not schools are succeeding. We must know "Who is best?" We desire not merely some effective intervention strategies for schools in need, but demand to know "Who is worst?" This impulse—what I shall call the "comparative imperative"—leads to some of the more silly errors in educational analysis. In general, these errors are what every beginning statistics student would call a "distinction without a difference."

The question before educational analysts is similarly complex: Given myriad data about different schools, how do we determine whether the differences between them are sufficiently meaningful to say that one school is a "success" and another one is in need of immediate and decisive intervention? The traditional responses to this question are distinctly unsatisfying, as they merely rank or label schools without offering insights about how to improve performance. Ranking assumes that the bottom third of schools is different from the middle and upper third, as schools are ranked based on test scores and other data.

Step 6. Measure What You Value: Systemwide Indicators

The next step in the development of a comprehensive accountability system is the selection of systemwide indicators. These indicators represent the most broadly shared values and goals of a school system. Every school, regardless of the focus of its curriculum, the economic status of its students, or any other unique characteristics, must share a common commitment to a core set of objectives. A district's goals and objectives represent those steps that the system believes will help it close the gap between its vision of where it would like to be and the current reality of where the district is. Although strategies and leadership techniques may vary widely from one school to another, every school within a system shares—or should share—some common values and objectives. Systemwide accountability indicators put these common values and objectives into measurable terms that the district can then use to assess its progress toward meeting its goals.

How many systemwide indicators is enough for the average accountability system? Although those people assigned to implement an accountability system can be tempted to bury their readers with data, my recommendation is that systemwide indicators be limited to only five or six indicators for each level of school. That is, five or six indicators for elementary, perhaps a separate five or six indicators for middle schools, and another five or six indicators for high school.

The demographic data about schools—student population, percentage of students eligible for free and reduced lunch, number of students receiving special education instruction, and so on—should be included as part of an accountability report because they can provide important contextual information for the reader. These data are *not accountability indicators,* however, but are only included in the report to provide an analytical frame of reference. As a matter of equity for schools and high expectations for students, it is imperative that all schools—regardless of the demographic characteristics of their student populations—choose systemwide indicators that are challenging and rigorous. This does not occur when a district establishes different student performance expectations based on the demographic characteristics of a school.

Where is the best place to start when selecting systemwide indicators for the district's accountability plan? An important first step is to conduct a "data inventory." This inventory should include every measurement that is routinely taken by a school system, including assessment and test data, attendance, tardiness, suspensions, expulsions, surveys, course enrollment, and so on. Such an inventory will likely leave Accountability Task Force members surprised by the sheer volume of data collected by its school district. Some of this data may be useful for the accountability system; a great deal of it will not. The best way to discern the meaningful useful data from the irrelevant information is this question: Will this piece of data help a classroom teacher change curriculum, assessment, and instruction and thus improve student performance? The Task Force may determine that some critically important pieces of information are missing and that some additional data gathering or additional analyses of existing data may be necessary. For example, data from classroom assessments and building analyses of teacher assessment practices can be vital pieces of information, but these are frequently omitted from traditional accountability systems.

Step 7. Strategies for Achieving the Values: School-Based Indicators

School-based accountability indicators are specific and measurable actions at the classroom and building level. These indicators reflect specific strategies that are linked to the achievement of systemwide goals. The best school-based indicators reflect the unique needs and challenges of that building environment. They are selected based on a careful analysis of assessment and diagnostic information, as well as the professional judgment of teachers and leaders within each individual school. When properly used, school-based indicators provide continuous feedback to leaders, teachers, and students. Whereas the systemwide goals are typically district and state assessments that are tracked only once a year, the school-based indicators represent classroom and building-level data that can be tracked every month or more frequently.

School-based indicators are more than the typical list of goals from school improvement plans, strategic plans, or other documents. The essence of effective school-based indicators is *synergy*. In the context of educational accountability, the synergy between systemwide indicators and school-based indicators occurs when their combined use creates a greater effect than the use of those two indicators in isolation.

How does synergy work? Typically, accountability systems report isolated variables (test scores) and teachers are implored to improve those results in the future. The implication is that the path to improvement is some change in effort or practice by students and teachers, but little is known about improvement until the next year's test scores are provided. By producing information on the strategies and practices teachers use to achieve student results, school-based indicators have a direct impact not only on instructional practices but also on the student achievement measured in systemwide indicators.

How many goals and school-based indicators are too many? It is impossible to be precise and prescriptive, but it is fair to say that when the number of goals exceeds 10, the faculty and leadership risk losing their focus. My colleagues at the Center for Performance Assessment work with outstanding school systems that have four to six systemwide goals and a similar number of school-based indicators for each building. If, for example, the goals focus on reading, writing, math, and safety, the implication is not that science, social studies, music, art, and physical education are unimportant. Rather, there is a clarion call for all those activities to avoid the typical curriculum isolation that prevails in so many schools and pull together in a concerted effort to achieve those four goals. In these schools, the physical education teachers help students in measurement, the social studies teachers encourage student writing skills, and the science teachers improve problem-solving abilities. The music teachers do not lose their aesthetic value and artistic commitment because they help students with fractions, vocabulary, and critical thinking skills. In other words, the focus on a few school-based indicators does not diminish the importance of curriculum and activities, but it elevates every activity, unit, and class into a critically important academic activity.

Step 8. Communicating About Accountability: Reports to Stakeholders

District Accountability Reports

The annual accountability report begins with a district summary and includes individual information on each school in the system. The district summary includes the systemwide indicators as well as an analysis of trends in school-based accountability reports. The district summary should focus on five key questions:

- What were our goals?
- What was our performance compared to our goals?
- What was our performance compared to previous years?
- What strategies worked well to improve student achievement?
- What does the information in the accountability report tell us about how to improve student achievement?

Recently, a superintendent asked, "Why don't we just report the test scores? After all, that's what people really want to see." There is an understandable impatience with long reports and unnecessary detail. These five questions, however, lie at the heart of effective accountability. The omission of important information in the district summary is an invitation to superficiality and oversimplification. We should be guided by Einstein's maxim that "things should be as simple as possible, but not more so."

School Accountability Reports

Some school systems recoil at the idea of including information about individual schools in a district accountability report. I heard one senior administrator say, with a straight face, "If people in the community want information about individual schools, then they can just go to the schools and get it." The reluctance to share individual school data as part of the district report is based on the fear that the public would compare schools to one another and develop rankings that would hurt the morale of the faculty and students. The strategy of the administrators appeared to be that failure to disclose school data would lead journalists and other curious members of the public to give up and presume that all is well with the state of education. In fact, in the minds of education critics, the line between reluctance to share data, however benign the motives, and "hiding" information with sinister intentions is a thin one. When the information does come out, as it inevitably must, those prone to compare and sort and rank schools will do so with gusto, their methodology unencumbered by logic or analysis. As a consequence, school leaders are invariably better served by providing complete information—not simply the test scores to which the indolent journalist may resort but all of the systemwide and school-based indicators, along with brief narratives on each school.

Step 9. Lead by Example:
Central Office Accountability

The central office, where the work of senior administrators and staff is carried out, must be included in a comprehensive accountability system. Most superintendents have heard this pointed question: "What do all those people in the central office do, anyway?" When a board of education member poses this question during a budget discussion, the ax can fall quickly on central office functions that may be important but have been invisible to the public and policymakers. The use of a comprehensive accountability system gives central office functions visibility, responsibility, and accountability. Such a system can serve not only as an effective advocate for central office functions, but it can also send the clear message to teachers and community members that the senior administrators in the district are held accountable in the same way that teachers and principals are held accountable.

The architecture of the central office accountability system is parallel to that of the school accountability system. The central office accountability system contains three levels: common goals, departmental goals, and narrative descriptions of the performance of the department. Central office common goals are established by the Accountability Task Force and approved by the school board. Central office departmental goals are established by the accountability team of each department of the central office, and reviewed by the Accountability Task Force. For the sake of clarification, common goals for the central office accountability system should not be confused with systemwide goals for the school accountability system. Although each has an effect on the other, they are two different sets of objectives.

Measurement of central office goals includes a focus on both absolute achievement and yearly improvement. The common goals generally focus on consistent measurements of absolute achievement, whereas the departmental goals focus on yearly improvement.

Step 10. The Holistic Accountability Cycle: Use Accountability to Improve Teaching, Learning, and Leadership

The ultimate value of any accountability system is the use of the data from the system to improve teaching, learning, and leadership. This can be achieved in a series of data-driven decision-making seminars that focus on these questions: What do the accountability reports tell us about our students at this school or in this class? What specific areas of achievement represent our greatest strengths? What specific areas of the curriculum represent our greatest challenges?

What do the accountability reports suggest about the relationship between teaching and leadership strategies and student achievement? In order to respond to this question, it is necessary to consider more than the data from a single school. The educators and administrators of one school must consider not only their own data but also the accountability information from all other schools in the system. This broad sharing of insights allows a constructive and open-ended discussion of effective instructional practices.

What do the accountability reports suggest about the impact of leadership practices on student learning? It is not uncommon for administrators to review the relationship between poverty and student achievement. At the most superficial level, they consider the correlation between the percentage of students eligible for free or reduced lunch and test scores. A consideration of leadership practices from the accountability report would require a deeper inquiry. If, as is quite common, administrators determined that the schools with higher percentages of students from low-income families also had higher percentages of teachers who lacked appropriate certification, then it is a leadership decision—the allocation of teaching resources—not merely the economic status of the students that must be considered.

This final step of the holistic accountability process is by far the most critical. It provides meaning, context, and reward for all the hard work that went into the creation of the entire accountability system. The successful implementation of this step allows school leaders to do more than "hold schools accountable" but, rather, maintains their focus where it belongs: the improvement of student achievement.

Conclusion

The skeptical reader might pose this challenge: "This is a lot of work! Why should we go through this drill when the public and, for that matter, our state department, our board, and the local newspaper are just going to look at test scores anyway?" The notion of holistic accountability does not discuss the demands of the state department, newspaper, or board. However, it is essential to recall that these are not the only stakeholders in educational accountability. The students, parents, teachers, and communities served by our schools are also stakeholders. They benefit from an accountability system that provides more than a list of scores and ranks. These 10 steps do not ignore state and local demands, but the holistic accountability system will put state and local demands in context. It will provide meaning and rationality to the existing accountability systems. It does not replace the requirements now in place, but it provides the context and value that is sadly lacking in almost every educational accountability system currently in use.

CHAPTER 8

Rhetoric and Reason: Communicating About Educational Accountability

When poet Robert Burns penned his famous line "The best laid schemes o' mice an' men/Gang aft agley" (Bartlett, 1919), he might have been reflecting on an accountability report from a Scottish school. No matter how careful the system design, no matter how inclusive the membership of the Task Force, and no matter how artistic the graphic design, a poorly constructed accountability report will undermine all of the efforts of an otherwise terrific accountability system. This chapter describes some of the pitfalls in communicating about educational accountability and suggests ways to avoid them.

Communication: Multiple Paths and Multiple Channels

First, let us dismiss the idea of the "accountability report" as a singular document. In a complex system with multiple stakeholders, successful communication depends on multiple channels of communication. Some readers will relish every detail that can be provided to them, whereas others will resent anything more than a brief executive summary. Some people want information on the entire school system, whereas others are strictly concerned with a single building. Some readers will demand comparative data and ranking, whereas others will understand and even embrace a standards-based approach to reporting educational achievement. An effective accountability reporting system requires a consideration of all these needs.

The starting point for this conversation is a single set of information: the comprehensive accountability report. This is a document that typically includes three pages for each school building. The first page shows the performance and progress of the school on the systemwide goals. The second page identifies the school-based strategies that were employed by the school and provides measurements of achievement and progress for each of those goals. The third page contains the narrative that provides a qualitative description of the educational environment of the school and offers clarity and insight into the quantitative information on the two preceding pages (please see Appendix A for examples). The comprehensive accountability report also includes district-level analysis, along with insights that can be gained from an examination of the school-level data in the report. Ideally, this report is published annually and is available in print and on the school system's Web site. Any reporter, community member, or other interested party can never complain that information on educational accountability is unavailable or mysterious. The accountability report is comprehensive, meaningful, and user-friendly.

A variety of summaries should also be available. These include an executive summary that provides a brief overview of the major accountability system findings for the entire system on three or fewer pages. In addition, summaries for each individual school should be available. Finally, summaries on particular accountability findings should be regularly issued throughout the year. If the district finds, for example, that schools that used a particular reading program or that conducted frequent student writing assessments experienced significant gains in achievement, then research summaries should be published so that teachers, parents, administrators, and students understand that there is a sound local research rationale for changes in teaching and learning strategies. These research summaries can offer a useful combination of case studies of single classrooms and schools and systematic analyses of large groups of students. No single piece of research resolves complex issues of educational practice, but a mountain of evidence that includes qualitative case studies and comprehensive quantitative multivariate analyses should provide far more information than the common assertions such as "research says that" or "I tried this last year and so it must work." The greatest contribution that any accountability system report can offer is not merely a reflection on the past but a useful guideline for the future.

In addition to using a variety of media (printed reports, summaries in newspapers, Internet Web sites, etc.), the school system that wishes to have comprehensive communication will consider publishing the accountability report in the most commonly spoken languages of its community. In addition, the reading level of the narrative portion of the report should be screened for vocabulary and complexity so that it is accessible to the widest possible audience. Finally, a series of "Reports to Stakeholders" should be made to specific community groups and parent organizations by a variety of school administrators, teachers, and parent leaders. The consistent themes of these public reports should be that accountability is an open process, there are no secrets, the reports are widely available, and of course, that the purpose for all of this emphasis on accountability is the continuous improvement of student achievement.

The "Customer" Is Not Always Right

With the advent of the quality movement in education, some theorists have extended the business metaphor one step too far. The taxpayers, they argue, are the "customer" and, after all, "the customer is always right." In fact, this notion is neither true in business nor in education. Customers of successful businesses and professional practices are always treated with respect, but they are not always right. If the customer insists that the pork chops are really tenderloin and asks the butcher to correct the label, the butcher will not do so because there is an obligation to all customers for accurate labeling that is more important than catering to a single customer's insistence on an inaccurate point of view. Professionals in medicine and law maintain successful practices by dealing courteously with their patients and clients, not by becoming obsequious. In fact, professionals have taken oaths that explicitly govern their conduct, even when that conduct is inconsistent with the wishes of a customer who desires something that is medically, ethically, or legally wrong. So it is in the profession of education. There are thoughtful and decent community members, parents, and, in the vernacular of the business metaphor, customers, who have strong opinions about what the enterprise of education should be, how it should be conducted, and how accountability for it should be reported. Because many of these thoughtful and decent people vehemently disagree with one another, it is impossible that each of these customers is right. This leaves the school leaders, policymakers, and Accountability Task Force members to ponder the question, "What's worth fighting for out there?" (Fullan & Hargreaves, 1998).

What's Worth Fighting for Out There?

In the context of educational accountability, some issues are worth the fight required to stand one's moral ground. The first issue worth fighting for is accuracy. This may not seem to be much of a debatable proposition until we confront the delicate issue of ranking and labeling. As the previous chapter on standards indicated, the problem with ranking and labeling has nothing to do with hurting the feelings of people who have low ranks and shabby labels. The problem is that labels and ranks are inherently inaccurate. They suffer from the statistical and logical error commonly referred to as a distinction without a difference. This occurs when the labeling system identifies a school with a score of 80 or higher as satisfactory and those schools that are below 80 as unsatisfactory or whatever local term is used to describe less-than-satisfactory performance. The logical problem is that this system presumes a meaningful difference between a school with a score of 80.1 and another school with a score of 79.8, and such a presumption of meaningful difference is rarely accurate. The same is true between a school that is in the "Top 10" by rank and an 11th-ranked school. There is a great apparent difference in label, but a meaningless difference in actual performance. The problem, therefore, is that labels and rankings may be popular, but they are frequently inaccurate, conveying insinuations of success or failure that are not supported by the actual evidence on student achievement within those schools. These inaccuracies affect not only schools with low ranks or unsatisfactory labels. Indeed, some of the most pernicious impacts of the ranking and labeling in many accountability systems is the inappropriate complacency that it breeds in the schools that have poor curricula, inept teaching strategies, low scores, and ineffective leadership but, the accountability systems happily report, are not quite as wretched as some other schools and thus can bask in their comparative glory.

More important, the labeling and ranking so common in accountability systems does little to inform better decision making. In fact, some school systems and states use their labels and rankings for precisely the wrong reason, taking away resources from schools that need them the most. Labels and ranks invite error and inaccurate inference. Because many people are so accustomed to labels and ranks, they may ask with an air of incredulity, "Without labels and ranks, what educational accountability information *will* we have?" The response to this challenge is that in a holistic accountability system citizens and stakeholders have something far more valuable than the superficiality of box scores and rankings: They have information that can be used to improve student learning through improved professional practice and better leadership decisions.

Strategic Communication of Accountability Information

In addition to the public accountability reports that are available to any citizen, schools should also consider some strategic communication using accountability information that will have more limited distribution. For example, policymakers and community leaders can use accountability data from their own school system and from other school districts with holistic accountability systems to share information about the impact (or the lack of impact) of programs, curricula, professional development offerings, technology offerings, alternative schedules, and other matters that require the significant investment of resources. Parents can benefit from accountability reports that are designed to show the progress of their own children. The class average or school rank is far less relevant to most parents than the performance of their own children. Such a report can provide an important supplement to the traditional report card and provide school leaders with a check on the consistency between evaluations of academic achievement that are reflected in the accountability system and the view of academic achievement as reflected on a report card.

Accountability reports for teachers can radically transform their perception of accountability systems from the typical "gotcha!" to thoughtful inquiry into the antecedents of student performance. One of the most meaningful teacher reports is an accountability report that considers the length of time that students are with a teacher, group of teachers, or school and the performance of those students in academic and behavioral variables. This is particularly essential for teachers working in schools with high rates of mobility. Although the average scores for such schools are rarely illuminating, a report that shows the performance of students who have worked with a teacher for a full year, or particularly for a longer time, will frequently make clear that when the teacher has the opportunity to provide a long-lasting and consistent influence on a child, the results are positive. In those rare cases where the accountability report shows that the longer a child is with a teacher, the worse that child performs, then administrators have an obligation to make direct observations of teaching practice and identify the root causes for such performance.

Strategic communication of accountability reports should also consider prospective students, their families who are new to the area, and businesses that are seeking to recruit employees to the area. It is commonly asserted that some of the most frequent users of educational accountability information are real estate agents who use that data to help prospective homebuyers identify the place they wish to live. Indeed, I have conducted Internet Web searches using the words "California educational accountability" and can inadvertently be on a real estate site within a few clicks of the mouse. Although some educators resent the use of accountability in such a commercial manner, we should consider this an opportunity to replace information that is typically fragmentary and sometimes inaccurate with accountability reports that are comprehensive, fair, and meaningful. Every school has a story to tell about its staff and students, and an accountability report strategically directed toward prospective new students is an excellent way to convey that message. Private schools routinely create brochures to attract prospective students and entice their families; public schools should use accountability information to do the same.

Accountability Information on the Internet

A number of school systems and states have provided accountability information, including narrative descriptions of each school, on the Internet. As a frequent visitor to these accountability sites, let me offer some suggestions for school systems considering the creation or update of their Web sites to include accountability data. First, use summaries wherever possible. Although some readers may be interested in the full text of accountability documents, most Internet searchers want quick access to information that has already been briefly summarized.

Second, for the person who wishes to have more extensive accountability data, provide information in the most user-friendly format available. My personal preference is for documents that can be easily loaded into a spreadsheet such as Microsoft Excel or a database such as FileMaker Pro. The Web sites of the states of Virginia (www.pen.k12.va.us) and Wisconsin (www.dpi.state.wi.us) are excellent examples.

Third, make sure the Web site addresses the information that parents and students want to know. The Memphis City Schools Web site (www.memphis-schools.k12.tn.us) is exemplary in this regard, providing clear answers to the simple question, "What is my child studying in school this week, and how can I help?" The site contains references for parents and teachers to support and supplement the specific curriculum that is the focus for every school for the next six weeks.

Fourth, consider student-designed Web sites for information on individual schools. The best feature of student sites is not only the opportunity for the display of student ability but also the display of the quality of work that is expected of students at that school. No oration by the principal about high expectations can equal the impact of multiple samples of exemplary student work.

Conclusion

In the final analysis, leaders in public and private education systems cannot choose to avoid accountability. They can only choose the kind of accountability system they will have. Will it be an implicit accountability system, full of questionable assumptions and inaccurate inferences? Will it be a fragmentary accountability system that provides a list of test scores but no elaboration about how those scores were achieved? Will it be a system that demoralizes and humiliates staff members and students, confirming every negative preconception of education? Will it be a system that is so complex that few people pay attention to it or take it seriously? Will it be a system that panders to popular demands and sacrifices accuracy and comprehensiveness on the altar of contemporary whim and political expediency? We cannot choose to avoid accountability; we can only choose whether to do the job badly or to do the job well.

Holistic accountability provides a better alternative. The design for accountability systems offered in these pages is neither a "one size fits all" nor a "cookie cutter" approach to this exceptionally complex challenge. If you persisted thus far, the bad news is that your work has only begun. The creation of a holistic accountability system will require at least six months of collaborative effort. The good news is that if you are reading this book, you are very likely a hard-working teacher, administrator, board member, or political leader, and you are going to be quite busy anyway. Thus the choice to use your time wisely, investing it in the creation of an educational accountability system that is fair, meaningful, and comprehensive, is a splendid use of your time and intellectual energy. You can replace the accountability system in your classroom, school, district, or state with one that is committed to the improvement of student achievement. You can transform a subject that is laden with acrimony to one that is constructive, insightful, and inspiring. You can reject superficiality and inaccuracy and embrace comprehensiveness and precision. You can find the antecedents of excellence in your own back yard. In sum, you can create holistic accountability. The children we serve and the communities in which we live deserve no less.

Appendix A
Sample Accountability Reports

T he following pages contain sample accountability reports for three school levels (elementary, middle school, and high school), as well as a sample Central Office Department Report.

The contents of these sample reports is based on information from actual schools and assimilated to form a comprehensive report. As such, they should not be taken as prototypes for the "perfect" report. Instead, they are intended to provide an example of how these schools blended qualitative and quantitative indicators to provide useful, concise information for their stakeholders.

An effective accountability report should have three key elements: systemwide indicators, school-based indicators, and qualitative descriptions, referred to in these reports as Tiers 1, 2, and 3, respectively. Demographic and enrollment information are included solely for informational purposes and should not be construed as indicators in their own right.

The purpose of the accountability report is to provide useful information in these areas to assess performance and to make decisions based on data. Based on the system established, the report should clearly communicate to all educational stakeholders the progress of the students, schools, and district.

The Tier 1 and Tier 2 data must have clear and understandable explanations for the numbers reported. Test scores should include information about how the tests are scored and when the tests are administered—both grade level and time of year. In addition, the report should include demographic and statistical data by school, such as enrollment, and a breakdown by ethnicity, socioeconomic level, and so on.

An essential element of a comprehensive accountability report is the narrative description in Tier 3. Many schools and school systems include numbers and statistics, but few think to provide a context for those numbers. Including a narrative in your report provides your readers with the background information they need to interpret the numbers.

The following sample accountability reports include one for each school level: elementary school, middle school, and high school. Notice that although each report is made at the school level, each school's progress toward systemwide indicators is reported.

Table A.1 Wellington Elementary School Annual Accountability Report, June 1999

General Information		Demographics	
Address:	1495 S. 3rd St.	Female:	53%
Phone:	487-8723	Male:	47%
Principal:	Thomas Greene		
		African American:	74%
Enrollment		Hispanic:	2%
Total:	365	White:	24%
K:	65		
1:	67	Regular Ed.:	91%
2:	54	Special Ed.:	9%
3:	59	LEP:	0%
4:	62		
5:	58	Free/Reduced Lunch:	49%

Systemwide Indicators: Tier I

Indicator	System Goal	System Score 1998-99	School Score 1997-98	School Score 1998-99	% Change
% of students who scored proficient or higher on State Criterion-Referenced Test in Reading	80	74	68	72	5.8
% of students who scored proficient or higher on State Criterion-Referenced Test in Mathematics	55	52	40	50	25
% of students with attendance rates of 90% or higher	85	87	84	7	−9.5
% of students who have been in school since September 1998 who scored proficient or higher on district 4th-grade, 4-point scoring guide for writing	80	71	62	64	3
% of African American students who perform at or above their grade level in reading	85	70	66	75	13.6

Table A.2 Wellington Elementary School Annual Accountability Report, June 1999, Page 2

School-Based Indicators: Tier 2

Indicator	School Score 1997-98	School Score 1998-99	% Change
Increase number of parent volunteer hours	652 hours	704 hours	7.9
Increase number of community service projects undertaken by the school	3 projects	5 projects	66
Increase number of computers available for student use at all grade levels	30 computers	40 computers	33
Increase number of students who participate in school-sponsored conflict resolution/reduction workshops	142 students	204 students	43
Increase the number of students performing at or above expected grade level or age on a teacher-made language arts assessment	165 students	212 students	28
Increase the number of students who read 8 books and share something they learned orally, artistically, musically, or by doing multimedia presentation	60 students	134 students	123
Increase the number of writing samples scored by someone other than the student's classroom teacher	56 writing samples	115 writing samples	105

Table A.2b Wellington Elementary School Annual Accountability Report,
June 1999, Page 3

School Narrative: Tier 3

The 1998-99 school year was a success in many respects for Wellington Elementary. The school was also presented with some challenges. Our academic performance based on the state 4th-grade test improved in the areas of reading and math.

Reading: A new reading program was implemented during the 1998-99 school year in the 3rd and 4th grades. Every student in the 3rd and 4th grades participated in this program for approximately five hours per week from January through May, 1999. In this program, teacher-made performance assessments for reading were given every two weeks. These assessments included multiple methods of demonstrating learning.

Mathematics: Wellington began an intervention program for students with low performance in mathematics. The students attended tutor sessions with a certified teacher for 45 minutes once a week. In addition, the new computers we received gave more students the opportunity to practice their math skills on the *Math Lab* program. The program was so much fun that the students were asking to practice on it during the lunch period.

Parent Involvement: Parents were encouraged to participate in many activities. The 4th and 5th grade teachers held a special night for student arts and crafts with help from many parents. The Parent Teacher Association at Wellington held two fund-raisers this year to raise money for the resource center. Our school is attempting to improve the attendance rates by increasing parent involvement.

Conflict Resolution: We hired a new school counselor this year, Dr. Marcia Wembley, who organized weekly conflict resolution workshops. Students were required to attend their first workshop, and subsequent participation was on a volunteer basis. Our hope is that this will help them grow into better and more peaceful citizens.

Table A.3 Greenleaf Middle School Annual Accountability Report,
June 1999

General Information		*Demographics*	
Address:	132 Schoolhouse Way	Female:	54%
Phone:	486-0846	Male:	46%
Principal:	Sharon Mozier Jones		
		African American:	36%
Enrollment		Native American:	2%
Total:	813	Hispanic:	14%
6:	265	White:	48%
7:	301		
8:	247	Regular Ed.:	86%
		Special Ed.:	11%
		LEP:	3%
		Free/Reduced Lunch:	43%

Systemwide Indicators: Tier 1

Indicator	System Goal	System Score 1998-99	School Score 1997-98	School Score 1998-99	% Change
% of students who scored proficient or higher on State Criterion-Referenced Test in Language Arts	65	42	45	41	−8.9
% of students who scored proficient or higher on State Criterion-Referenced Test in Mathematics	40	43	35	41	17
% of students who scored proficient or higher on State Criterion-Referenced Test in Science	50	58	60	62	3.3
% of students with attendance rates of 90% or higher	85	83	89	92	3.4
Final GPA for students with 90% or higher attendance rates	3.0	2.8	2.4	3.1	29

Table A.4 Greenleaf Middle School Annual Accountability Report,
June 1999, Page 2

School-Based Indicators: Tier 2

Indicator	School Score 1997-98	School Score 1998-99	% Change
Increase the percentage of minority students who meet or exceed the district standard on the district writing performance assessment	52%	45%	−15
Increase the percentage of students directly involved in the performing arts	10%	15%	50
Increase the percentage of parents who attend parent-teacher conferences	46%	42%	−8.7
Reduce to zero the number of incidents involving violence, drugs, alcohol, and gangs	18 incidents	14 incidents	−22
Increase the percentage of middle-school trained and licensed teachers	47%	62%	31
Increase the percentage of students who engage in direct interaction with community/business partners on science projects	13%	31%	19
Increase the percentage of students enrolled in pre-algebra and/or algebra courses	26%	31%	19

Table A.4b Greenleaf Middle School Annual Accountability Report,
June 1999, Page 3

School Narrative: Tier 3

I am proud to report that the 1998-99 school year was a very good one for Greenleaf Middle School.

Our increase in proficient or higher State Math scores is due in part to the hiring of two teachers, Mr. Ludwig and Mrs. Ramirez, who are licensed in teaching mathematics at the middle school level. Their understanding of their field and patience with their students made a huge difference in the students' understanding of and enthusiasm for math.

I cannot, unfortunately, report such good scores in state and district language arts. Last year, we agreed to get rid of our existing language program, *Language Is Power*, in favor of a new one, *Newman's Reading and Writing*. I fear that the decision was not the wisest, because the new program did not aid the children in understanding the material as well as they have in past years. We will look again for a new program this summer.

With regard to the decrease in parents attending parent-teacher conferences, a change of staff in our main office caused several notices for said conferences not to be mailed. As a result, fewer parents were informed of the fall conferences this year than last year. We have agreed to monitor the main office more closely and to aim for lower personnel turnover in the future.

Although violence and substance abuse were down this year from last, none of us can let down our guard. I believe that part of the decrease has to do with a particularly troublesome group of 8th graders who left after the 1997-98 school year to go to high school.

We added a new music teacher to the department this year, Miss Long, whose expertise in and enthusiasm for jazz is contagious. After her choir's first in-school performance, students lined up to ask to participate in her after-school choir.

Table A.5 Bainbridge High School Annual Accountability Report,
June 1999

General Information		*Demographics*	
Address:	2636 Foundation Rd.	Female:	49%
Phone:	485-9673	Male:	51%
Principal:	Jeanine Howard		
		Native American:	3%
Enrollment		African American:	58%
Total:	1758	Hispanic:	8%
9:	512	White:	31%
10:	478		
11:	416	Regular Ed.:	89%
12:	352	Special Ed.:	7%
		LEP:	4%

Systemwide Indicators: Tier 1

Indicator	System Goal	District Score 1998-99	School Score 1997-98	School Score 1998-99	% Change
% of students who scored proficient or higher on State Criterion-Referenced Test in Language Arts	80	67	72	70	−2.8
% of students who scored proficient or higher on State Criterion-Referenced Test in Mathematics	70	65	64	72	9.4
% of students who scored proficient or higher on State Criterion-Referenced Test in Science	65	66	57	67	17
% of students with an attendance rate of 90% or higher	75	72	74	73	−1.4
% of 9th-grade students meeting algebra requirements	80	67	56	61	9

Table A.6 Bainbridge High School Annual Accountability Report,
June 1999, Page 2

School-Based Indicators: Tier 2

Indicator	School Score 1997-98	School Score 1998-99	% Change
Increase the number of career-oriented projects and activities	9	15	66
Increase the percentage of students who successfully meet standards in college preparatory classes	30%	35%	16
Increase the percentage of students who pass the High School Competency Examination required for graduation on the first trial	46%	52%	13
Increase the percentage of high school graduates who enroll in a four-year college or university	33%	43%	30
Decrease the number of violent incidents in the school	39	30	–23
Increase the percentage of students who score proficient or higher in writing, as demonstrated by student portfolios	65%	70%	7.7

Table A.6a Bainbridge High School Annual Accountability Report,
June 1999, Page 3

School Narrative: Tier 3

Overall, the 1998-99 school year was one of great academic progress for Bainbridge High School. Many of our school-based indicators were structured so that, once met successfully, they helped us achieve other indicators. An excellent example of this was our goal for more students to meet standards in the college prep classes. A change in personnel and curriculum seemed to help, as did making some of the study guides and materials available online. And because these classes were mainly math and science oriented, students who had taken them did better on the state test in those subjects.

I believe that the college prep courses also helped more students to successfully complete the High School Competency Examination. During this exam, we also strove to make the environment much less stressful than it has been in recent years, offering more frequent breaks and making available an assortment of snacks to help test takers keep their energy up.

Our exciting increase in the number of four-year college-bound students is due to the forward thinking of the senior class counselor, Ms. Dickinson. Ms. D. was finally approved this year to set up three computers with Internet access in her office, so that students could come in to research and apply for colleges, scholarships, and grants. Students became aware of the availability and ease with which they could plan their futures, and did so accordingly.

I would like to credit the school board for planning this year's school calendar so that the breaks were more evenly distributed and we never had to go too long without one. I have noticed that the longer kids have to go without a break, the more irritable and short-fused they become. Giving students a chance to rest their bodies and minds helped them avoid potential physical conflicts.

I also believe that the new schedule was responsible in part for the better GPA of the kids who were present at least 90% of the time. They were better able to concentrate on their studies.

Sample Central Office Report: Departmental Narrative

The departmental narrative gives the superintendent, board, and public the "story behind the numbers." Issues of morale, community volunteerism, direct work with schools and students, and a host of other activities that may not be evident in the sterile numbers of other reports can be highlighted in the departmental narrative. In the example that follows, the recreation department of the central office is able to tell a compelling story and show readers the relationship between this central office function and student achievement.

Every department has a story to tell, and neither budget numbers nor employee counts tells that story completely and accurately. A one-page narrative allows every department to proactively respond to the question, "What do those people in the central office do, anyway?"

Wakefield Public Schools Recreation Department

The Recreation Department completed the year with programs involving 3,802 youths in 34 summer programs and another 18 programs during the school year. As the numerical data in our report indicate, we completed the year 1.5% under our budget, experienced no serious accidents, and four minor student injuries. The activities of the Recreation Department have had a more significant impact on this community than the raw numbers may reflect.

Student Attendance

Improved student attendance has been an important goal of the district. Whereas the average attendance rate for the district is 89%, the average attendance rate of students participating in recreation programs during the school year exceeds 95%. The average attendance rate of summer school students was 78%; for those students participating in the summer recreation program, the average attendance rate was more than 90%. Although few people would associate the Recreation Department with academic achievement, it is fair to say that the students we serve are exposed to excellent adult role models and a consistent emphasis on attendance and good citizenship. Although our recreation specialists may not be certified teachers, they certainly have an impact on attendance and, as a result, on achievement.

Community Service

Eagle Crest High School has implemented a community service program as part of its school accountability program. Student and staff volunteers from Eagle Crest supported our five professional staff members in the Recreation Department. These volunteers collectively contributed more than 700 hours to serving students in recreation programs. In addition, our services expanded this year to include services to physically challenged students. Twenty-two students with physical and developmental disabilities participated in our regular recreation activities; the Department provided logistical and training support for Special Olympics in which another 56 students participated.

Professional Development

Two of our staff members completed their college degrees with majors in education. Although they continue to be employed by recreation services, they hope to find positions in the district physical education program. Whichever schools are lucky enough to get these outstanding professionals will each gain a "first-year" teacher with more than 10 years of experience in the Recreation Department. We have also provided professional development opportunities to district employees through our "Healthy Lunch" series. Our staff provides important information while the food service staff provides a carefully prepared healthy lunch for participants. Our classes for employees include stress reduction, stretching, weight training, fitness, and personal health.

Appendix B
Resources for Accountability Systems

The information contained in this appendix is intended to assist stakeholders and Accountability Task Forces in researching existing accountability systems to better design one of their own. It is by no means a comprehensive compilation of all material on educational accountability but should instead be viewed as a starting point. The list was current as of early 2001, but if the contact information is no longer accurate, please call the International Center for Educational Accountability at 1-800-844-6599, or visit our Web site at www.edaccountability.org. There are frequent updates and additions to the accountability information listed there. Please also refer to the list of references in this volume, as many of the books and articles to which I have referred in the text are useful sources for anyone interested in educational accountability. Uncited sources of interest are listed in the Bibliography.

Organizations

American Association of School Administrators
    1801 North Moore St.
    Arlington, VA 22209-1813
    (703) 528-0700
    www.aasa.org

Annenberg Institute for School Reform
    Brown University
    Box 1985
    Providence, RI 02912
    (401) 863-7990
    www.aisr.brown.edu

Brookings Institution
    1775 Massachusetts Ave. NW
    Washington, DC 20036
    (202) 797-6000
    www.brook.edu

Carnegie Foundation for the Advancement of Teaching
555 Middlefield Rd.
Menlo Park, CA 94025
(650) 566-5100
www.carnegiefoundation.org

Education Trust
1725 K St. NW, Suite 200
Washington, DC 20006
(202) 293-1217
www.edtrust.org

International Center for Educational Accountability
1660 S. Albion St., #1110
Denver, CO 80222
1-800-844-6599
www.edaccountability.org

Mid-Continent Research for Education and Learning (McRel)
2550 S. Parker Rd., Suite 500
Aurora, CO 80014
(303) 337-0990
www.mcrel.org

National Association of Secondary School Principals
1904 Association Dr.
Reston, VA 20191-1537
(703) 860-0200
www.nassp.org

National Education Association
1201 16th St. NW
Washington, D.C. 20036
(202) 833-4000
www.nea.org

U.S. Department of Education
400 Maryland Ave. SW
Washington, D.C. 20202-0498
1-800-USA-LEARN
www.ed.gov

Web Sites

Center for Performance Assessment
www.makingstandardswork.com

Council of Chief State School Officers
www.ccsso.org

Education Week on the Web
www.edweek.org

Educational Accountability
www.educationalaccountability.com

National Center for Fair & Open Testing
www.fairtest.org

National Staff Development Council
www.nsdc.org

The No Excuses Campaign/The Heritage Foundation
www.noexcuses.org

Public Broadcasting Systems Online
www.pbs.org

re: Learning by Design
www.relearning.org

School Choices: The Citizen's Guide to Education Reform
www.schoolchoices.org

Teachers College Record: The Voice of Scholarship in Education
www.tcrecord.org

References

Achilles, C. (1999). *Let's put kids first, finally: Getting class size right.* Thousand Oaks, CA: Corwin Press.

Alaska Department of Education and Early Development. (1997a). *Standards for Alaska's administrators* [Brochure]. Juneau, AK: Author.

Alaska Department of Education and Early Development. (1997b). *Standards for Alaska's teachers* [Brochure]. Juneau, AK: Author.

Answers in Riverview Gardens. (2000, September 14). [Editorial]. *St. Louis Post-Dispatch* (Five Star Lift Edition), p. B6.

Archer, J. (1999). Sanders 101. *Education Week, 18*(34), 26-28.

Archer, J. (2000). State teacher policies tied to student results. *Education Week, 19*(17), 3.

Bartlett, J. (1919). *Familiar quotations.* Boston: Little, Brown.

Bracey, G. (1999). The ninth Bracey report on the condition of public education. *Phi Delta Kappan, 81*(2), 147-168.

Bracey, G. (2000). The tenth Bracey report on the condition of public education. *Phi Delta Kappan, 82*(2), 133-144.

Coleman, A. L. (2000). None of the above. *Education Week, 19*(43), 42-45.

Durbin, D. (1999, November 9). Parents want legislature to take MEAP scores off transcripts. *Associated Press Newswires.*

Fullan, M., & Hargreaves, A. (1998). *What's worth fighting for out there?* New York: Teachers' College Press.

Guskey, T. R. (2000). *Evaluating professional development.* Thousand Oaks, CA: Corwin Press.

Guskey, T. R., & Bailey, J. M. (2000). *Developing grading and reporting systems for student learning.* Thousand Oaks, CA: Corwin Press.

Haycock, K. (1998). Good teaching matters: How well-qualified teachers can close the gap. *Thinking K-16, 3,* 1-16.

Haycock, K., Barth, P., Jackson, H., Mora, K., Ruiz, P., Robinson, S., & Wilkins, A. (Eds.). (1999). *Dispelling the myth: High poverty schools exceeding expectations.* Washington, DC: The Education Trust.

Henry, T. (2000, May 30). Ex-Xerox star turns to business of school reform: Book attacks "complacency," urges broader definition of "public." *USA Today,* p. 9D.

Ingersoll, R. (1999, March). The problem of underqualified teachers in American secondary schools. *Educational Researcher, 28*(2).

Janey, C. B. (2000). Pathways to high school success. *Education Week, 19*(43), 68, 45.

Johnston, R. C., & Viadero, D. (2000). Unmet promise: Raising minority achievement. *Education Week, 19*(27), 1, 18-19.

Kaplan, R. S., & Norton, D. P. (1996). *The balanced scorecard: Translating strategy into action.* Boston: Harvard Business School Press.

Kaplan, R. S., & Norton, D.P. (2000). *The strategy-focused organization: How balanced scorecard companies thrive in the new business environment.* Boston: Harvard Business School Press.

Marzano, R. (2000, July 19). Paper presented at the National School Conference Institute's Principals' Institute, Broomfield, CO.

Marzano, R., & Kendall, J. S. (1998). *A theory-based meta-analysis of research on instruction.* Aurora, CO: Mid-continent Research for Education and Learning.

Milwaukee Public Schools. (1999). *1998-99 Accountability report.* Milwaukee, WI: Author.

Neill, M. (1998). High stakes tests do not improve student learning. *FairTest Examiner, 12*(1).

Noble, J. (1999). What helps or hinders students' educational achievement? *American College Testing Program Information Brief, 99*(2). [On-line]. Available: www.act.org/research/briefs/99-2.html

Ohanian, S. (1999). *One size fits few: The folly of educational standards.* New York: Heinemann.

Popham, W. J. (2000). *Testing! testing: What every parent should know about school tests.* Boston: Allyn & Bacon.

Reeves, D. B. (2000a). *Accountability in action: A blueprint for learning organizations.* Denver: Advanced Learning Press.

Reeves, D. B. (2000b). Effective accountability: Clear answers for common sense questions. *Thrust for Educational Leadership, 129*(4).

Reeves, D. B. (2000c). Essential transformations for the secondary school. *NASSP Bulletin, 84*(620).

Sandham, J. L. (2000). State teacher-bonus plan catches Florida district short. *Education Week, 20*(10), 23, 27.

Sandowski, M. (2000). Are high-stakes tests worth the wager? *Harvard Education Letter, 16*(5), 1-5.

Weak tests drive math, science curricula. (1998, Spring). *Fair Test Examiner,* (12), 2.

Wiggins, G. (1988). *Educative assessment.* San Francisco: Jossey-Bass.

Bibliography

Darling-Hammond, L., & Sykes, G. (Eds.). (1999). *Teaching as the learning profession: Handbook of policy and practice.* San Francisco: Jossey-Bass.

Falk, B. (2000). *The heart of the matter: Using standards and assessment to learn.* Portsmouth, NH: Heinemann.

Gardner, H. (1999). *The disciplined mind: What all students should understand.* New York: Simon & Schuster.

Grissmer, D., Flanagan, A., Kawata, J., & Williamson, S. (2000). *Improving student achievement: What state NAEP test scores tell us.* Santa Monica, CA: RAND Corporation.

Kohn, A. (1999). *The schools our children deserve: Moving beyond traditional classrooms and "tougher standards."* Boston: Houghton Mifflin.

Lemann, N. (1999). *The big test: The secret history of the American meritocracy.* New York: Farrar, Straus & Giroux.

Marzano, R. J., Kendall, J. S., &. Cicchinelli, L. F. (1998). *What Americans believe students should know: A survey of U.S. adults.* Aurora, CO: Mid-continent Research for Education and Learning.

McNeil, L. M. (2000). "Creating new inequalities: Contradictions of reform." *Phi Delta Kappan, 81*(10), 728-734.

Pfeffer, J., & Sutton, R. I. (2000). *The knowing-doing gap: How smart companies turn knowledge into action.* Boston: Harvard Business School Press.

Ravitch, D. (2000). *Left back: A century of failed school reforms.* New York: Simon & Schuster.

Reeves, D. B. (1997). *Making standards work: How to implement standards-based assessments in the classroom, school, and district.* Denver, CO: Advanced Learning Press.

Rooney, C., & Schaeffer, B. (1998). *Test scores do not equal merit: Enhancing equity and excellence in college admissions by de-emphasizing SAT and SAT results.* Cambridge, MA: FairTest.

Schmoker, M. (2000). The results we want. *Educational Leadership, 57*(5), 62-65.

Schmoker, M., & Marzano, R. (1999). Realizing the promise of standards-based education. *Educational Leadership, 56*(6), 17-21.

Senge, P. (Ed.). Cambron-McCabe, N., Lucas, T., Smith, B. Dutton, J., & Kleiner, A. (2000). *Schools that learn: A fifth discipline field book for educators, parents, and everyone who cares about education.* New York: Doubleday.

Stigler, J. W., & Hiebert, J. (1999). *The teaching gap.* New York: Free Press.

Teachers wanted. (2000, March 20). *Newsweek,* p. 76.

Westgaard, O. (1999). *Tests that work: Designing and delivering fair and practical measurement tools in the workplace.* San Francisco: Jossey-Bass.

Index

CORWIN
PRESS

The Corwin Press logo—a raven striding across an open book—represents the happy union of courage and learning. We are a professional-level publisher of books and journals for K–12 educators, and we are committed to creating and providing resources that embody these qualities. Corwin's motto is "Success for All Learners."